BLACK CULTURE & GENERATIONAL POVERTY

A Historical, Economic, and Sociological Analysis

By

GERMINAL G. VAN

Winner of the 2021 Best Indie Book Awards for Socioeconomic History

Amazon Digital Services, LLC

To Elise,

This book is a work of historical, economic, and sociological analysis. No part of this book may be reproduced, stored in a retrieval system, or transmitted in any form or by any means, including electronic, mechanical, photocopying, microfilming, recording, or otherwise (except for that copying permitted by sections 107 and 108 of the United States Copyright Law and expect by reviewers for the public press), without written permission from the Publisher.

Copyright©2022 by Germinal G. Van
All Rights Reserved

Published by Amazon Digital Services, LLC

authorgerminalgvan@gmail.com

ISBN: 979-8-406-837-689

SELECTED BOOKS PUBLISHED BY GERMINAL G. VAN

Reflection on Identity Politics

Democratic Socialism On Trial

Income Inequality & Economics

Classical Liberalism in Africa

The Economic Development of West Africa in the Twenty-First Century

The Economic Condition of Black America in the Twentieth Century

Political Decisions & Economic Outcomes

Limited Government & Political Decentralization

A Statistical Inquiry into the Cost of Healthcare

The Economic Policy of Thomas Jefferson

TABLE OF CONTENTS

About the Author	9
Preface	11
Introduction	17
1 – How is Poverty Measured?	27
2 – Racism & Generational Poverty in the Black Community	49
3 – Black Culture and the Welfare State	75
4 – Black Culture & Counterproductive Habits	89
5 – Black Culture, The Victimhood Mentality & Critical Race Theory	119
6 – Black Culture & the Stock Market	137
7 – Black Culture & Infrastructures	157
8 – Black Culture, Crime & Generational Poverty	171
9 – Propositions to Improve Black Culture	197
10 – Wealth Creation in the Black Community	211
References	225
List of Figures and Tables	253

ABOUT THE AUTHOR

Germinal G. Van is an economist, political scientist, and award-winning author. He is the author of more than twenty books. His major publications include *The Economic Condition of Black America in the Twentieth Century*, *A Statistical Inquiry into the Cost of Healthcare in America*, and *The Economic Policy of Thomas Jefferson*. He also authored more than a dozen papers on technical economics. He published with *The Journal of Economics and Econometrics* and on other research platforms.

Mr. Van was born and raised in Abidjan, Côte d'Ivoire, West Africa. He pursued his primary and secondary education in Abidjan where he obtained his high school diploma in 2010. That same year, he immigrated to the United States to pursue his undergraduate studies in political science at the Catholic University of America. He graduated from that institution with a bachelor's degree in 2014. He subsequently enrolled in 2015 in the Graduate School of Political Management at the George Washington University. He graduated from that institution with a master's degree in political management in 2017. Mr. Van holds a non-degree certificate in mathematical statistics from Duke University that he earned online via Coursera.

Mr. Van focuses his work on Economic History, Public Choice Theory, Mathematical Economics, and Econometrics. His research mainly concentrates on the empirical research side of the social sciences. *Black Culture & Generational Poverty* is his twenty-third book.

PREFACE

This book is by far the most controversial subject I have ever written about. I anticipate, but without any apprehension or fear, the surge of criticisms that will revolt against this book. I am perfectly aware that this book will not leave anyone indifferent, and it is even the goal.

I expect the majority of Black Americans who will read this book to vehemently criticize it and even call me names, given their political affiliation. Indeed, those who define themselves as liberal in the modern context of the American political landscape (a term that I unequivocally reject due to its erroneous use), will assert that this book was written in a preconceived fashion with a single-minded ideology, which has the sole purpose of upholding the conservative values of our society, which they find outmoded. Those who lean more towards American conservatism will necessarily argue that I am one of them because we share the same opinions and vision. One thing is certain, this book will polarize public opinion on this subject. My aim, though, is in no way to polarize public opinion. My goal, in writing this book, is to address and dissect a sensitive subject as logically and rationally as possible in order to enlighten collective minds and instigate social change.

As a human being, I am bound to have opinions on almost every subject. Consequently, I can come across as biased. However, it is important to clarify that this book is not an opinion book. It is a book of empirical research where the scientific method is used systematically and rigorously.

The scientific method is value-free. It is the process wherein we confront our prejudices with reality by using empirical data to obtain concrete results that describe what is rather than what we want it to be. That being said, I do not offer my personal opinion in this book. On the contrary, I offer the results of my statistical research to the public. Thus, those who will read this book, especially the ones who ideologically do not share my views, will therefore not be able to claim that the arguments put forth in this work are unsubstantiated. The facts remain the facts whether we agree with them or not. Our opinions and feelings can never change the essence of the truth.

Those who dispute the results of my research, which is their right to do so, are therefore invited to use the scientific method in an attempt to falsify the entirety of my hypothesis, which suggests that the root cause of the scourge of generational poverty in the Black community is not based on racism or the legacy of slavery, but it is rather based on the counterproductive habits that Black Americans have adopted and defined them as their culture. I do not, however, believe that the results of my research are definitive. They are certainly substantial and consequential in disproving the common narrative that dominates the mainstream media and the Black community.

As society evolves, certain assumptions of my general hypothesis will have to be tested again at some point in time. I leave this task to the forthcoming social scientists who will carry the torch on this specific subject.

Germinal G. Van

January 2022

"Everybody has asked the question, and they learned to ask it early of the abolitionists, 'What shall we do with the Negro?' I have had but one answer from the beginning. Do nothing with us! Your doing with us has already played the mischief with us. Do nothing with us!"

Frederick Douglass

INTRODUCTION

Overview of the Book

The general premise of this book is not new. Indeed, this hypothesis had already been put forward by Chicago economist, Dr. Thomas Sowell. Dr. Sowell repeatedly argued through his numerous works, that Black Americans have been poor longer than they should have been, not because of the legacy of slavery or racism, but because of a set of counterproductive behaviors that have set back the Black community. Thus, the hypothesis defended in this book is not groundbreaking. What is, on the other hand, pathbreaking in this book is the new elements added to this analysis to reinforce our thesis. We extended significantly on the work already built by Dr. Sowell. We have developed a comprehensive analysis that recapitulates the correlation between Black American culture and generational poverty.

The United States is a multi-racial; multi-ethnic society founded on cultural pluralism where all the communities of the national population have had learned to coexist under the same ideal. Of all the communities that make up American society, Asian and White communities are the most prosperous while the Hispanic and Black communities continue to struggle to become socioeconomically stable.

The common denominator of all these communities aforementioned is poverty. As a matter of fact, each of these communities has experienced poverty at some point in America's history. The White community was very poor at the dawn of the nineteenth century since the United States then was an agricultural society. It was not until the 1820s that the White community began to make significant economic and financial progress thanks to the Industrial Revolution that was exported to America from Great Britain. The Asian community was very poor at the twilight of that century. But in the twentieth century, they began to also make considerable economic and financial progress to even become today the most economically-advanced community of the national population. The Hispanic and Black communities, on the other hand, have been lagging. The Hispanic community has done important economic progress over the last few decades. The Black community remains the community whose economic progress is immensely slow and tardive. The Black community is generally described as an economically and financially strangled community. This economic and financial asphyxiation has persisted in the Black community for generations while in other communities, the poverty they encountered and experienced at some point was described as situational or temporary poverty.

The fundamental question we all ask ourselves is why is the notion of generational poverty associated with the Black community? The official answer to this question is that racism and the legacy of slavery are the cause of generational poverty within the Black community. Economists have argued that racism and slavery played a role in limiting and denying economic opportunities to Blacks. For example, the redlining policies prevented Blacks from owning real estate in affluent neighborhoods, which compelled them to live in ghettos and, therefore, lacked economic opportunities to improve their living condition. Historians have argued that generational poverty is the result of racism being institutionalized for many decades. And this institutionalization of racism has been passed down to the younger generations who had to live in a society where they have been denied opportunities and equal treatment under the law because of their skin color. For example, Black people's right to vote was denied because of institutional racism. Sociologists have argued that slavery played a psychological role in the mind of Black people by making them believe that they were inferior to other races, especially to Whites. This belief of racial inferiority complex has pushed Blacks to isolate themselves rather than trying to integrate into American society whose cultural and social standards are based on Western culture.

These explanations provided to justify the official response to our inquiry are not unsubstantiated. Racism and slavery indeed played a role at some point in the economic and social evolution of the Black community. This is undeniable. These explanations provided now raise new questions that need answers. Hence, this compels us to ask to what period in time were racism and the legacy of slavery the most relevant in preventing Blacks from advancing? Can we objectively claim that racism and the legacy of slavery continue to play a major role in the collective behavior of the Black community in this twenty-first century compared to the 1950s and 60s?

The explanations provided by social scientists (economists, historians, and sociologists) to justify the impact of racism and the legacy of slavery on the collective behavior of the Black Americans suggest that the Black community is a deterministic community. Determinism is the doctrine that all events, including human action, are ultimately determined by causes external to the will.[1] If the Black community is a deterministic community based on the explanations provided by social scientists, it implies that Black Americans have no free will. Meaning that regardless of the actions they have committed, they are never responsible for its consequences since determinism rejects the fact that the one who initiated the act cannot be held responsible for the consequences of that act since that act was caused by external elements independent of his will. Interestingly enough, the American criminal justice system was theoretically designed and structured on consequentialism.[2] The American criminal justice system is founded on the belief that man is responsible for his deeds and therefore must be held accountable for the consequences of his deeds. This belief is what pioneered the prevalence of the rule of law in the United States.

When we look at the statistics, according to the Federal Bureau of Prisons, Black Americans represent 38.2 percent of inmates while Whites represent 57.8 percent. Of course, Whites have a higher percentage because they

---

[1] *Oxford Dictionary*

[2] Consequentialism is the doctrine that the morality of an action is to be judged solely by its consequences. Consequentialism argues that actions have consequences and the person who has initiated the act is therefore responsible for the consequences of that act initiated.

represent a larger percentage of the national population. The Black community is 13 percent of the national population while 38.2 percent within those 13 percent are incarcerated. On theoretical grounds, an imprisoned person is incarcerated because he or she has committed a crime and is therefore held responsible for the crime committed. In practice though, it is far more complicated than that and the criminal justice system has proven to be defective on numerous occasions. Nonetheless, if Blacks are incarcerated in prisons the same as Whites and other ethnic groups, it implies that Black Americans do have free will after all because they are held accountable for their actions. If, for example, a Black teenager robs a local grocery store in his neighborhood but then gets apprehended by a White police officer, who is then held responsible for the outcome? Should we blame the White police officer who is simply doing his job, which is to maintain law and order in the streets, or the Black teenager who was aware beforehand of the consequences of his actions if he gets caught but decide to pursue the robbery anyways? Was it a racist act by the White police officer to apprehend and arrest the Black teenager who deliberately committed a crime? If the Black teenager decided to rob a local grocery store while knowing upfront the consequences of his actions if apprehended, then can't we assert that this teenager has free will? We believe the answer to this series of questions is obvious to anyone who uses basic common sense.

In this book, we argue that the scourge of generational poverty in the Black community is not a social phenomenon of deterministic nature as suggested by social scientists, but rather a social phenomenon of consequentialist essence. The inability of the Black community to generate generational wealth consistently is rooted in the pernicious behavior of Black culture, not in racism or the legacy of slavery. In short, it is endogenous rather than exogenous. Generational poverty in the Black community is perpetuated by the counterproductive deeds of Black culture. What is Black culture? The definition of Black culture will be postulated in this analysis.

To support our arguments, we relied on a set of qualitative and quantitative empirical techniques to demonstrate that our hypothesis is scientifically valid. The statistical techniques we used in the book are not illustrated in the main content of the analysis, they are relegated to the footnotes. Only the results of our econometric analyses are part of the main content. The reason why the statistical methods we used in this book are not part of the main content is to facilitate the understanding of our analysis to the average reader who may lack a background in statistics and mathematics. Our objective is to make this book as accessible as possible.

Organization of the Book

This book contains ten chapters. The first chapter entitled "How is Poverty Measured?", focuses on the examination of poverty in the United States. It analyzes the characteristics of poverty and how it is applied to ethnic groups.

The second chapter is titled "Racism and Generational Poverty in the Black Community." As the title suggests, this chapter investigates the relationship between racism and generational poverty. In analyzing this relationship, we concluded that racism is not the causation of generational poverty in the Black Community. We arrived at that conclusion by using a set of qualitative empirical methods.

The third chapter is titled "Black Culture and the Welfare State." In this chapter, we investigated the impact of the welfare state on Black culture. Since Black culture cannot be measured quantitatively, we performed a qualitative assessment to demonstrate how the policies of the welfare state have harmed the Black community culturally and socially.

The fourth chapter is entitled "Black Culture and Counterproductive Behavior." This chapter is certainly the most preponderant of all chapters in this book because it analyzes the central idea of our general hypothesis. It explains how counterproductive habits eventually became endogenous to the Black community. It elucidates how Black Americans progressively embraced these habits and how these habits contributed to stagnating the economic and social advancement of the Black community. This chapter concluded that these habits are the cornerstone of the sustentation of generational poverty in the Black community.

The fifth chapter is entitled "Black Culture, the Victimhood Mentality, & Critical Race Theory." This chapter articulates the reasons why Black culture focuses on victimhood mentality, and how this defeatist mentality has become the cornerstone of critical theory, which is now promulgated in American public schools.

The sixth chapter is entitled "Black Culture and the Stock Market." This chapter explains why most Black Americans do not invest in the stock market whereas the stock market is one of the most profitable platforms to create generational wealth.

The seventh chapter of this book is titled "Black Culture and Infrastructures." This chapter analyzes the lack of infrastructures in the Black community and how this lack of infrastructure prevents the community from advancing economically and socially while other communities have developed their infrastructures to ensure that the pillars of their community are strong. This chapter stressed that infrastructures are the foundations of a community's sustainability and that a community is doomed to stay in poverty if it neglects to invest in its infrastructural aspect.

The eighth chapter of this book is entitled "Black Culture, Crime, and Generational Poverty." This is perhaps the second-most crucial chapter of this book because it addresses the issue of crime in the Black community, an issue that has been perhaps the mightiest issue that has hindered the Black community for generations. It argues that crime in the community is based on the lack of trust among Blacks and the high rate of criminality and incarcerated Black people is an engine of generational poverty.

The ninth chapter is titled "Propositions to Improve Black Culture." This chapter offers a set of recommendations that could put a halt to the cycle of generational poverty in the Black community and help them improve the community if they embrace these recommendations.

The tenth and last chapter of this book is entitled "Wealth Creation in the Black Community." This chapter explains what it takes to create wealth and how a community that focuses on creating wealth by creating value will inevitably prosper in almost all aspects of society.

1. HOW IS POVERTY MEASURED?

How to reduce poverty is the fundamental question that all lawmakers ask themselves and pass policies accordingly. Indeed, poverty is the central theme of the social sciences when it comes to the material conditions of individuals living in civil society. How to reduce poverty does not have a single approach according to lawmakers. It all depends on the political side and ideology that each political leader defends.

As was aforementioned in the introduction of this book, the Black community is the poorest community in the United States in terms of revenue per capita. And the plague of generational poverty has become a sort of a cultural identity for the Black community. It is assumed that Black Americans are de facto poor. When, for example, Black students apply to college, they are given preferential treatments on the basis that they are poor. School administrators automatically assume a Black student who applies to college necessarily comes from a rough neighborhood and needs extra help to catch up with others.

In American culture and its social system, a social correlation has been established between an individual's skin color and his social status. This relationship is based on the assumption that Whites are generally wealthy, educated, and well-established in society while Blacks are generally poor, lack education, and fill out penitentiaries. Thus, individuals are stereotyped according to their ethnic group rather than their individuality. Being a White individual of European descent does not mean that one is unconsciously wealthy and well-established, just as being Black of African descent does not systematically mean that one is poor and a criminal. There are poor White people and there are rich Black people.

The dynamic between poverty and wealth is not based on the ethnicity of individuals but on the behavior that each individual adopts in order to change his material condition. How to reduce poverty remains the question that needs an answer. But in order to answer this question, it is important to ask what is poverty, what creates poverty, and how it is measured? Poverty cannot be reduced unless it is measured, and the objective of this chapter is to assess how poverty is measured.

1. What is Poverty and what creates it?

a) Definition and Concept of Poverty

Have we ever asked ourselves what creates brightness or darkness? We do not think so. We know that day and night exist they each occur every single day since planet earth exists. The day is the absence of darkness just as night is the absence of light. The same logic applies to the notion of poverty. Poverty is merely the absence of wealth while wealth is the absence of poverty. What creates poverty? Nothing creates poverty. Poverty is the starting point for any improvement of the material condition of humans. Poverty is the norm and wealth is the exception.

The United States was once poor, Europe was once poor, China was once poor, Japan was once poor, every country on earth was once poor. No society on earth was rich from its inception. All human societies started poor then became wealthy over time. The human species began in poverty. The question then we shall ask ourselves is what creates wealth? This answer will be more elaborated in the last chapter of this book, but the short and rapid answer to this question is that wealth is created through human capital when human beings used their skills, intelligence, and discernment to create economic value. Wealth is created when people are willing to pay for a product or service on the marketplace in exchange for its value. Individuals pay for value; they purchase elements that they believe are valuable to them. Hence a human being who earns an income is no longer poor. He may neither be rich nor wealthy, but he is surely not poor since to be poor, one must absolutely earn no income at all. By that definition, the poorest members of society are generally children since they do not earn an income until they are legally authorized to work.

b) *The Relativity of Poverty*

Poverty is comparative. It depends on certain parameters such as the standard of living of a given region, spending habits, and the savings propensity of each individual.

Suppose a person lives in San Francisco or somewhere near the Bay Area and earns $100,000 of gross income per year. Let us assume that this person lives in an affluent neighborhood where rents and property taxes are significantly high. Let us further assume that this person only pays rent. With federal and state income taxes combined, which is 33.3 percent[3], this person pays $33,300 annually in taxes and therefore has a net income of about $66,700 (this is even before health insurance, social security, and other social contributions are deducted from his annual gross income). Although this person earns $100,000 a year, which is way above the average national income per capita ($67,521 according to the U.S. Census), this person would be considered poor because of the cost of living[4] in the Bay Area which is far above his net income. It would, therefore, be quasi-impossible for this person to live comfortably in that area without worrying about making ends meet.

Let us now assume that this same person lives in Salt Lake City, Utah, and earns the same gross income ($100,000 a year) and still pays rent. While federal income tax remains at 24 percent, state income tax in Utah is set at 4.95 percent[5], which is 4.35 percent less than California's income tax. As federal and state income taxes are combined, this person pays $28,950 annually in income taxes and therefore has a net annual income of about $71,050 (like the previous hypothetical example, health insurance, social security, and other social contributions have not yet been deducted from his gross income). We see here that this person saved $4,350 just

---

[3] Federal income tax is 33% for individual making between $86,376 and $164,925 a year and California income tax is 9.3% for people making between $61,215 and $312,686 a year. (24% + 9.3% = 33.3%). Source: *U.S. Department of the Treasury*.

[4] Cost of living includes housing cost, food cost, gas cost, taxes, healthcare, clothing, education, transportation, entertainment...etc.

[5] Utah has a flat state income tax. Regardless of income bracket, every taxpayer living in Utah pays the same tax rate.

by living in Utah instead of California. Moreover, the cost of living in Utah is significantly cheaper than California's, which places this person among the most well-off people in Salt Lake City.

The thought experiment we utilized to illustrate the relativity of poverty shows us that poverty cannot be analyzed uniformly because there are too many parameters that intertwine and shape the meaning of poverty. The definition that we provided about poverty is the most objective and value-free definition. A $65,000 median household income can be more than enough in one location to live on while it might be far too insufficient to live on in another location. Hence the way poverty is defined by bureaucrats can sometimes be misleading and needs careful reassessment of its meaning.

2. The Two Types of Poverty: Situational Poverty and Generational Poverty

There are two basic types of poverty in a society. Situational poverty and generational poverty. Each type has impacted communities in many different ways. The substantive difference between these two kinds of poverty is that one is short-termed while the other is long-termed.

a) Situational Poverty

Situational poverty is a state of poverty generally caused by a sudden crisis or loss.[6] For example, the coronavirus pandemic has created a condition of situational poverty

---

[6] Rubenstein, Jennifer. "Pluralism and Global Poverty." *British Journal of Political Science*. Vol. 43, No. 4. (2013). pp. 775-797

for many Americans as we can see in figure 1.0. During that time, unemployment dramatically skyrocketed then fell to its original level as we can observe in figure 1.1. The coronavirus generated much temporary unemployment, mostly based on lay-offs. Situational poverty is characterized by a short-term span.

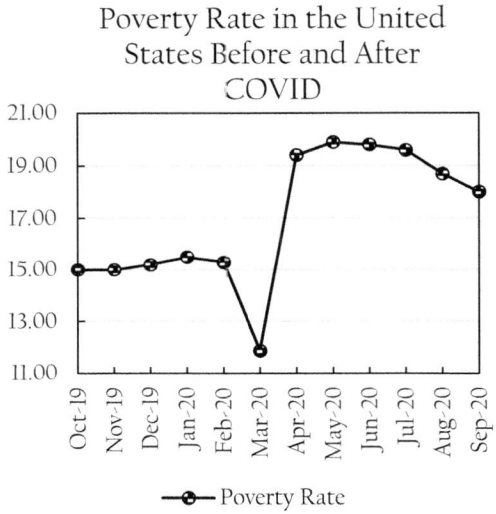

Figure 1.0. Source: U.S. Bureau of Labor Statistics

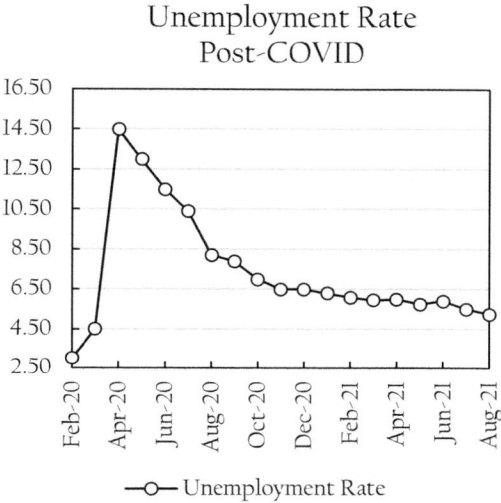

Figure 1.1. Source: U.S. Bureau of Labor Statistics

The main characteristic of this type of poverty is that it is deterministic. Sudden crises and unforeseen events are types of happenstances that humans do not and cannot control. Situational poverty is short-termed because the people who become poor under this condition are usually people with technical qualities that allow them to be eventually competitive in the labor market and hence, recover from their social downfall. Let us use a hypothetical example to illustrate our point.

Let us assume, for example, that a corporate lawyer has just been laid-off. Let us further assume that this lawyer is married and has a family. His wife holds a bachelor's degree but has not been working for more than five years. She chose to be a housewife, and therefore his family lives solely on his income. Finally, let us assume that this lawyer has only one year of professional experience in the legal industry as a practicing lawyer. Based on these three main assumptions, we can deduce that this family will endure situational poverty since his wife and children depend on his income, but he is no longer employed. Nevertheless, there are then three possibilities to remedy this situation. The first possibility is that the lawyer finds employment at another law firm, the second possibility is that his wife comes back into the workforce, and the third possibility is for the lawyer to simply start his own law firm.

The second possibility is the least realistic of all three because she has not been actively employed for at least five years. This gap in her employment history then has decreased her value and competitiveness in the labor market. From an employer's perspective, it is risky to employ someone who has been inactive for quite some time in the workforce. Her productivity will not be as high as those who have been actively working. And the cost of training will be more expensive for the employer because she will have to spend a lot of time updating her skill set for the job since she has not worked for so long. Moreover, despite her lack her continued skills and consistent productivity in the workforce, the employer must pay her a competitive wage. In short, she will be more of a liability than an asset for employers and this liability can be illustrated in the following graph.[7]

---

[7] DL = Demand for Labor; SL = Supply for Labor

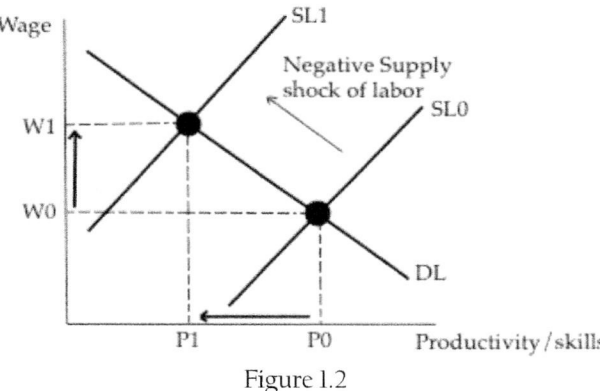

Figure 1.2

The third option is doable but not necessarily plausible because starting a law firm requires substantial financial capital, an established reputation, which this lawyer does not have since he has been only practicing law for a year and he does not have a strong track-record. Clients would not necessarily feel comfortable working with a lawyer who does not have sufficient practicing experience to handle complex legal matters, and they want a lawyer who can win complicated cases consistently for them. Hence, we consider the third option to be a long shot.

The first possibility is the most plausible and realistic of all three based on the urgencies that need to be met. Although the lawyer only has one year of experience as a practicing attorney, he will likely find a new job at another law firm because the legal field is a technical field that requires expertise. Lawyers are, by essence, experts at analyzing the law, and their legal training is one of the most technical programs in society. It is, therefore, remotely impossible for a licensed and practicing attorney to live in abject poverty in the long-term because his job as a lawyer will enable him to always find work since legal skills are skills that are constantly in demand. And this constant demand for legal services is illustrated in figure 1.4.[8]

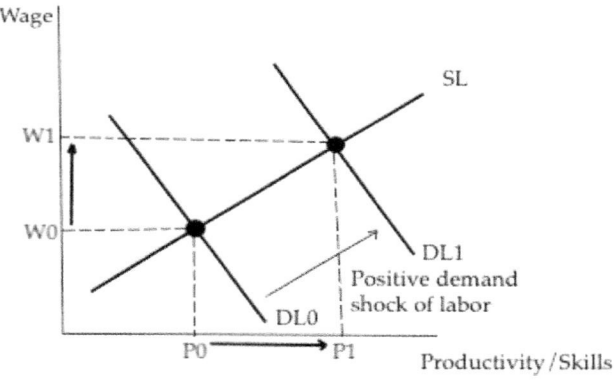

Figure 1.3.

The hypothetical example of the lawyer helped us understand that situational poverty is generally limited to individuals who have technical skills and work experience but have been victims of negative happenstances. These kinds of people cannot remain poor

---

[8] Ibid.

for too long because their value and professional experience are an asset to society's productivity.

b) *Generational Poverty*

The word *generational poverty* means that poverty is transmitted from one generation to another and so on. In this kind of condition, poverty becomes a perpetual cycle. The specific characteristic of generational poverty is based on the fact that it is initially deterministic but progressively becomes consequentialist over time.

One can be born in a poor family. This is a deterministic condition because no one chooses the family in which they are born and raised. But remaining poor is a consequentialist condition because one has free will and free will gives us the power to make choices on a daily basis to change our condition. In the American social culture, the term "generational poverty" is generally associated with the Black community. As we can see in figure 1.5., the Black community has the highest poverty rate according to the latest data released from the U.S. Census Bureau in September 2021.

U.S. Poverty Statistics by Race

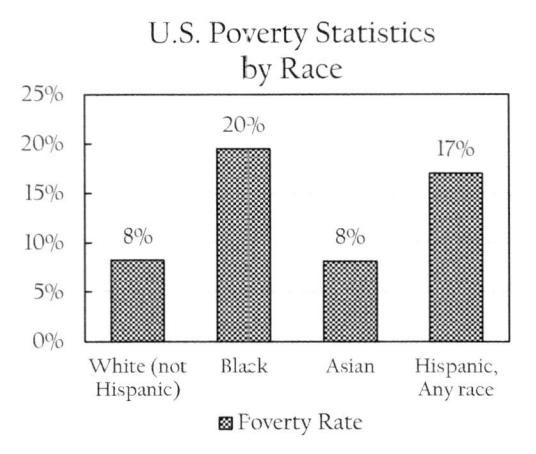

Race	Poverty Rate
White (not Hispanic)	8%
Black	20%
Asian	8%
Hispanic, Any race	17%

Figure 1.4. Source: U.S. Census Bureau

Wealth ownership in the United States has long been concentrated in the hands of a small minority of the population.[9] This fact is undeniable, but it is not unique to the United States. There is wealth inequality in every country that operates within a market economy system, and wealth ownership is generally concentrated within a small minority of the population. Since the early 1920s in the United States, the top 1 percent holders have consistently owned an average of 30 percent of total household sector wealth.[10] Some studies on wealth mobility have suggested that upward movement is rare and that eras of relative equality reflect deflated asset prices than they do improvements in the financial well-being of the majority of the population.[11] These studies

---

[9] Keister, Lisa A.; Moller, Stephanie. "Wealth Inequality in the United States." *Annual Review of Sociology*, Vol. 26. pp. 63-81.
[10] Ibid. p. 63
[11] Ibid. p. 63

have argued that during economic downturns, the distribution of wealth has appeared more equal.[12]

If the justification for generational poverty is linked to the fact that the top 1 percent owns more than 30 percent of total household sector's wealth, it means then that those who are victims of generational poverty are in no way responsible for their own continuance in this condition. This insinuates that income mobility is static, and people stay in the same income bracket indefinitely. This is, however, not true. Income mobility is not a static phenomenon, it is a dynamic phenomenon. Professor Thomas A. Hirschl of Cornell University and Mark Rank looked at forty-four years of longitudinal data regarding individuals from ages 25 to 60 to see what percentage of the American population would experience these different levels of affluence during their lives.[13] They found that 12 percent of the population will find themselves in the top 1 percent on the income distribution for at least one year.[14] 39 percent of Americans will spend a year in the top 5 percent of the income distribution, 56 percent will find themselves in the top 10 percent, and 73 percent will spend a year in the top 20 percent of the income distribution.[15] These statistics can be observed in figure 1.6.

---

[12] Ibid. p. 63
[13] Perry, Mark J. "Some Amazing Findings on Income Mobility in the U.S. including the Image of a Static 1 and 99 percent is False." *American Enterprise Institute.* (2017).
[14] Perry, 2017
[15] Perry, 2017

Percent of Americans Adults Who
Reached Various Income Distribution
Levels over a 44-Year Period

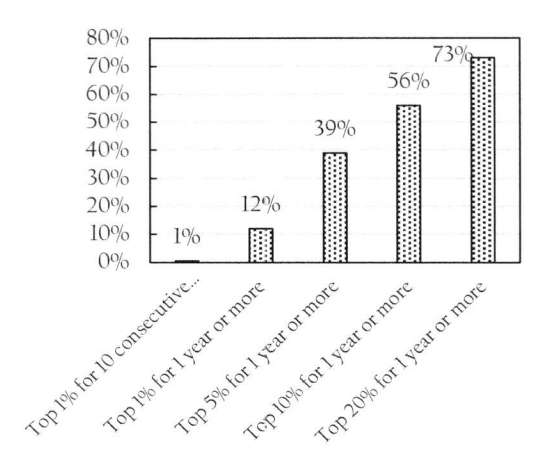

Bracket	Percent
Top 1% for 10 consecutive...	1%
Top 1% for 1 year or more	12%
Top 5% for 1 year or more	39%
Top 10% for 1 year or more	56%
Top 20% for 1 year or more	73%

▣ Percent of Income Distribution Levels

Figure 1.5. Source: Mark Rank and Thomas Hirschl

Our observation of these statistics suggests that it is not different people who are every time in different income brackets. It is the same people who have been moving upward. Let us not forget that work experience increases every year. As work experience increases, so is income. Individuals move from one income bracket to another after reaching a certain income threshold. The difference in ages of people in different income brackets—with the highest average incomes being among people 45 to 54 years old—strongly suggests that most of the people in upper-income brackets have reached that level only after rising from lower-income levels over the course of many

40

years.[16] In other words, they are no more of a lifetime class than are "the poor."[17] Much discussion of social mobility is based on the concept of "life chances"—the likelihood that someone born into given socioeconomic circumstances will grow up to achieve some given economic or occupational level.[18] Sometimes, causation is confused with blame, as when any attempt to point out factors in any social group which inhibit their progress is called "blaming the victim," presumably the "victim of society."[19]

Physical and mental handicaps beyond the individual's control may reduce the likelihood of utilizing various opportunities that are otherwise available in a given society.[20] Cultural values inherited socially rather than biologically, may also reduce the statistical probability of advancing in income or occupations, even when the opportunity to do so is available.[21] This is principally what characterizes generational poverty. A child raised in a home where physical prowess is valued more than intellectual prowess is unlikely to have the same goals and priorities as a child raised in a home where the reverse is true.[22]

---

[16] Sowell, Thomas. "Income Facts and Fallacies." *Economic Facts and Fallacies*, (2008). p. 138. Basic Books, New York. ISBN: 978-0-465-0-22-038.
[17] Ibid. p. 138
[18] Ibid. p. 146
[19] Ibid. p. 146
[20] Ibid. p. 146
[21] Ibid. p. 146
[22] Ibid. p. 146

To the extent blaming "society" is more or less the default setting for explaining differences in social mobility among income classes, ethnic groups, or other segments of society, this itself shifts attention away from internal factors which inhibit many individuals from using available opportunities.[23] By reducing awareness of such internal impediments to advancement, this approach reduces the chances of changes in such internal impediments—and thereby reduces the very chances for lower-income people to advance that these studies claim to be concerned about.[24] Consequently, it is fair to say that generational poverty has a more consequentialist rather than deterministic impact on the human condition since the individuals who live in such a condition are themselves recalcitrant to change their own behavior that is the actual cause in maintaining them in such poverty.

The concept of generational poverty is not strictly limited to Black Americans. It is also a phenomenon in Europe, especially with the Roma people. The Roma people are the most prominent poverty risk group in many of the countries of Central and Eastern Europe.[25] They are poorer than other groups, more likely to fall into poverty, and more likely to remain poor.[26] In some cases, Roma poverty rates are more than ten times higher than that of non-Roma.[27] For several interwoven reasons,

---

[23] Ibid. p. 147
[24] Ibid. p. 147
[25] Ringold, Dena; Orenstein, Mitchell A.; Wilkens, Erika. "Overview." *Roma in an Expanding Europe: Breaking the Poverty Cycle*, (2005). p. xiv. The World Bank. ISBN: 0-8213-5457-4
[26] Ibid. p. xiv
[27] Ibid. p. xiv

Roma poverty is rooted in their unfavorable starting point at the outset of the transition from planned to market economies.[28] Low education levels and overrepresentation among low-skilled jobs led to labor market disadvantages.[29] As a result, Roma have had more difficulty re-entering the job market than other groups and have become caught in a vicious circle of impoverishment.[30] Additional barriers include a lack of access to credit and unclear property ownership.[31] Combined with an overdependence on welfare, these factors create a poverty trap that precludes many Roma from improving their living conditions or starting their own businesses.[32]

According to a press release conducted by the European Union Agency for Fundamental Rights (FRA), 80 percent of Roma interviewed are at risk of poverty compared with an EU average of 17 percent; 30 percent live in households with no tap water and 46 percent have no indoor toilet, shower, or bathroom.[33] 30 percent of Roma children live in households where someone went to bed hungry at least once in the previous month; 53 percent of young Roma children attend early childhood education, often less than half the proportion of children their age from the general population in the same country; only 30 percent of the Roma surveyed are paid in work, compared with the

---

[28] Ibid. p. xiv
[29] Ibid. p. xiv
[30] Ibid. p. xv
[31] Ibid. p. xv
[32] Ibid. p. xv
[33] Staff, *80% of Roma are at Risk of Poverty, New Survey Finds*, European Union Agency for Fundamental Rights. (2016).

average EU employment rate for 2015 of 70 percent; 41 percent of Roma feel they have been discriminated against over the past five years in everyday situations such as seeking employment, at work, housing, health, and education; 82 percent of Roma are unaware of organizations offering support to victims of discrimination.[34] These numbers are striking. But we can see that the generational poverty that has prevailed in the Roma community is even worse than the one that has prevailed in the Black community in the United States.

The substantial difference between the Roma community and the Black American community is that the Roma community is geographically isolated from areas where economic activities are concentrated. Some Roma people do live in big cities but most of them living in these big cities are homeless. Most Romas live in remote areas, whereas Black Americans mostly live in dense cities where most of the economic activities take place. The Black American community is not isolated from American society like the Roma people are from Europe. Black Americans are part of America. They have access to more economic opportunities to improve their living conditions than Roma do. Then why is generational poverty is still striking in the Black community? This inquiry will be answered in the subsequent chapters of this book.

3. How is Poverty Measured?

We all know that poverty is the absence of wealth. Social scientists can at least agree on this elemental fact. Now

---

[34] Staff, 2016

how is this lack of wealth measured is the pinpoint of disagreement among social scientists and lawmakers. Indeed, the measurement of poverty is not a uniform procedure for all policy analysts and lawmakers. It depends on which country. Hence, each country measures poverty differently.

In the United States, poverty is measured by comparing a person's or family's income to a set poverty threshold or minimum amount of income needed to cover basic needs.[35] People whose income falls under their threshold are considered poor.[36] The U.S. Census Bureau determines poverty status by using an Official Poverty Measure (OPM) that compares pre-tax cash income against a threshold that is set at three times the cost of a minimum food diet in 1963 and adjusted for family size.[37] Income is defined by the OPM to include, before taxes, the following sources: earnings, unemployment and workers' compensation, social security, Supplemental Security Income, public assistance, Veteran's payments, Pensions or retirement income, interests, dividends, child support, educational assistance, and other miscellaneous sources.[38] In addition to using the OPM, the U.S. Census Bureau also uses the Supplemental Poverty Measure (SPM), which is another metric to measure poverty.

The SPM was introduced in 2010 to provide an alternative view of poverty in the United States that

---

[35] *How is Poverty Measured?* Institute for Research on Poverty. University of Wisconsin-Madison
[36] Ibid.
[37] Ibid.
[38] Ibid.

better reflect life in the twenty-first century, including contemporary social and economic realities and government policy.[39] Unlike the OPM, the SPM takes into account many government programs designed to assist low-income families and individuals that are not included in the OPM.[40] The following table shows the difference between the OPM and the SPM.

Poverty Measure Concepts: Official and Supplemental

Concept	OPM	SPM
Measurement Units	Families (Individuals related by birth, marriage, or adoption) or unrelated individuals	Resources units (official family definition plus any coresident unrelated children, foster children, and unmarried partners and their relatives) or unrelated individuals
Poverty Threshold	Three times the cost of a minimum food diet in 1963	Based on expenditures of food, clothing, shelter, and utilities
Threshold Adjustments	Vary by family size, composition, and age of householder	Vary by family size, composition, and tenure, with geographic adjustments for differences in housing costs
Updating Threshold	Consumer Price Index	Five-year moving average of

---

[39] Ibid.
[40] Fox, Liana; Burns, Kalee. "The Supplemental Poverty Measure: 2020." *U.S. Census Bureau.* P-60-275. (2021). Pp. 1-37

		expenditures on FCSU, 1 year lagged
Resource Measure	Gross before-tax cash income	Sum of cash income, plus noncash benefits that resource units can use to meet their FCSU needs, minus taxes, work expenses, medical expenses, and child support paid to another household

Table 1.0. Source: U.S. Census Bureau

The following figure shows the change in percentage of people in poverty by race using the Supplemental Poverty Measure from 2019 to 2020. As we observe the data, we see that the poverty rate decreases when using this metric (SPM). This is because the resource measure encapsulates a set of metrics that depict more accurately what individuals have and how they consume. The Supplemental Poverty Measure has a more holistic approach to measuring poverty than the Official Poverty Measure does.

According to the 2021 poverty guidelines provided by the Office of the Assistant Secretary for Planning and Evaluation and the U.S. Census Bureau, the poverty threshold for an individual is $12,880 while it is $44,660 for a family of eight people. In another country such as Colombia, this person who is considered poor according to American standards for making $12,880 a year would be making 51,109,772 Colombian pesos, which will make him a millionaire, and therefore be in the top 1 percent of Colombian society. This also shows how wealthy the United States is as a country. There is so much wealth produced, and economic opportunities created that the poverty level in this country would even make poor people millionaires in other countries.

Poverty Rate by Race from 2019 to 2020 using the Supplemental Poverty Measure

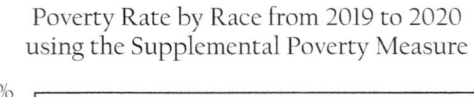

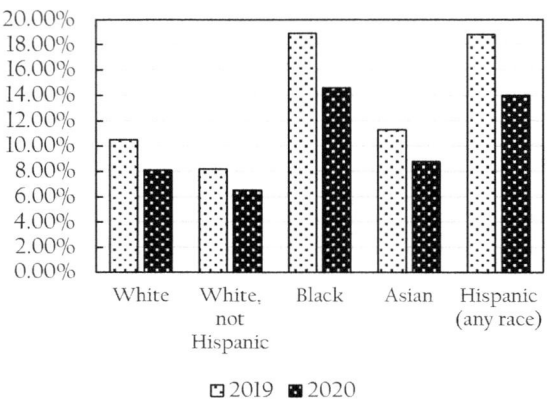

□ 2019 ■ 2020

Figure 1.6. Source: U.S. Census Bureau

2. RACISM & GENERATIONAL POVERTY IN THE BLACK COMMUNITY

It is important to say from the outset that racism has played a quintessential role in the structure of American culture and its socioeconomic system. The importance of this role does not mean that it was a positive role. The importance of racism here is related to its impact and consequences on American society.

We claim that racism was important in the sense that it has been an intrinsic part of American society since its inception. Indeed, racism has shaped American culture and society everlastingly in an indefinite number of ways. However, the reason why racism is such a deleterious, yet impactful social phenomenon is because it is an intrinsic element of multi-ethnic societies. Australia, Brazil, South Africa, Colombia, India, Uruguay, New Zealand, and Zimbabwe (former Rhodesia) are examples of multi-ethnic countries where racism has been part of their socioeconomic system.

1. An Understanding of the Functioning of Heterogeneous Societies

The common denominator of these aforementioned countries, including the United States, is that they are all heterogeneous societies. The principal characteristic of heterogenous societies is that the peoples that compose them are all from different cultures and racial origins, but they must coexist in the same place under the same laws and customs. Hence, heterogeneous societies are not multicultural because the cultures coexisting with one another are not equal. Heterogeneous societies are culturally pluralistic.

The coexistence of people in heterogenous societies has never been an easy task. At some point in the history of these heterogeneous societies, one racial and ethnic group exercised repressive power over groups of different racial backgrounds. For example, in South Africa, White South Africans, also known as Afrikaaners, despite being a minority in terms of population, exercised oppressive power over Black South Africans for decades until the early 1990s. In this oppressive system, minority White South Africans imposed their cultures, customs, laws, economic, and political systems on Black South Africans. India is another example where racial relations have been overwrought for many generations. According to the 2013 World Values Survey, 43.5 percent of Indians responded that they would not prefer to have neighbors of a different race.[41] Racism in India is called Brown racism where people are classified from the most light-skinned to the most dark-skinned and where antipathy toward dark-skinned and attraction toward light-skinned became customary.[42] In Brazil, the White majority also exerted a despotic system on other ethnic groups for many years.

---

[41] "A Fascinating Map of the World's Most and Least Racially Tolerant Countries." *The Washington Post. (2015).* ISSN: 0190-8286.
[42] Washington, Robert E. "Brown Racism and the Formation of a World System of Racial Stratification." *International Journal of Politics, Culture, and Society.* Vol. 4. No. 2. (1990). pp. 209-227

Heterogenous societies were built on power-struggle relations where one racial group with economic and political power, had to assert and impose its domination over the other ethnic-racial groups that did not have the financial, economic, and political resources to fight back. This is history and it is part of who we are as human beings. To have an established coexistence in a heterogeneous society like the United States, there must have to be periods of intense social struggles between peoples, and one must prevail over the other in order to establish a political, economic, and social system under which all the peoples of that heterogeneous society would agree to live by and consent to it.

2. Racism and Poverty in the United States

a) Institutional Racism

Racism is part of the integral history of the United States whether we like it or not. Racism and slavery are part of the American collective consciousness. As we explicated in the previous chapter, racism in the United is not based on skin color but on social class where it has been assumed that Whites are de facto rich and Blacks, Hispanics, and Amerindians are de facto poor.

Institutional racism is an embodiment of racism that suggests that the United States is structured as a society where political, legal, economic, and social institutions use racism as their main driving force to prevent the upward socioeconomic mobility of minorities in order to maintain White domination. Institutional racism has been mainly practiced in the Southern states during the Jim Crow era. In the 1930s, institutional racism was very much prevalent with the Homeowners' Loan Corporation where banks would determine a neighborhood's risk for loan default and redline neighborhoods that were at high risk of crime.[43] The federal government actively involved itself in institutional racism in the housing industry. In 1938, the *Underwriting Manual* of the Federal Housing Administration (FHA) cautioned home buyers: "if a neighborhood is to retain stability, it is necessary that properties shall continue to be occupied by the same social and racial group."[44] The manual recommended the use of restrictive covenants to keep out "inharmonious racial groups."[45] After constant pressure from civil rights groups, the federal government passed the Fair Housing Act of 1968, which attempted to prevent racial discrimination in the sale or rental of housing.[46] The passage of this act prompted many cities to adopt stringent zoning ordinances designed to keep low-income people and low-income housing out of the suburbs.[47]

Several studies led by prominent social scientists maintained that racism is the engine of poverty in minority ethnic groups (Asians, Blacks, Hispanics, and Amerindians). These studies have argued that racism, especially institutional racism, is the reason why these communities are at a critical disadvantage compared to Whites. In an article written by the *Huffington Post*, Angela

---

[43] Jones, Terry. "Institutional Racism in the United States." *Social Work*. Vol. 19, No. 2. (1974). pp. 218-225
[44] Ibid. p. 220
[45] Ibid. p. 220
[46] Ibid. p. 220
[47] Ibid. p. 220

Glover Blackwell who is the founder and the CEO of PolicyLink pointed out that more than one in four Blacks and Hispanics live below the poverty line; Hispanics saw the biggest jump in poverty (2.1 percent increase in poverty rate); biggest drop in real income was among Blacks and non-citizens (4.4 percent and 4.5 percent, respectively).[48]

According to Mrs. Blackwell, institutional racism is the primary device that caused these numbers to be outstandingly harmful to minorities, especially to Blacks and Hispanics. To curb the scourge of institutional racism, advocates of social equity such as Mrs. Blackwell have recommended using government power to enhance social justice as a means to equate economic outcomes between racial and social groups. The problem is that social justice is not real justice, and its means are not the means to curb poverty.

b) *Social Justice and The Politics of Poverty: An Impediment to the Advancement of Minorities*

The term "social justice" has become common currency in American political culture. It refers to the belief that everyone deserves equal economic, political, social rights and opportunities. It focuses on the equal redistribution of wealth, opportunities, and privileges.[49]

The central argument used by social justice advocates is that the government has the moral obligation to equalize

---

[48] Meehan, Deborah. "Structural Racism and Leadership." *Race, Poverty & the Environment.* Vol. 17, No. 2. (2010), pp. 41-43
[49] "Social Justice." *Oxford Languages.*

access to wealth, opportunities, and privileges for people, in particular for the disenfranchised, so that everyone could peacefully and equally benefit.

In abstract, this ideology seems morally right. In practice though, social justice has done more harm to those it intended to help and has hindered society's advancement as a whole. But to fully comprehend the reason why social justice has become an impediment to economic and social advancement; it is, first and foremost, judicious to fathom its origins.

The Origins of Social Justice

To understand social justice, we first need to define what justice is. Justice is a social organization bounded by legal rules, in which a third-party impartially adjudicates a dispute. And the purpose of adjudicating a dispute is to rectify a wrong deed committed on the person harmed whether it is an unjust deprivation of private property or bodily harm. Therefore, justice logically starts from the point that someone has been the victim of a wrong deed, and the third-party shall fix that wrong deed by returning to the victim, the adequate number of resources or elements that the victim has been deprived of or needs in order to repair the harm caused.

Social justice, however, is different. It is not actual justice because it is not a social institution like the family unit, education, or healthcare; are. It has therefore no legal grounds for its legitimacy. Social justice as a concept arose in the early 19th century during the Industrial Revolution and subsequent civil revolutions throughout

Europe, which aimed to create more egalitarian societies and remedy the capitalistic exploitation of human labor.[50]

Indeed, the concept of social justice is rooted in the Marxist theory of man-made exploitation. Advocates of social justice argue that social inequalities are based upon the fact that those who have access to resources, do so because they have deprived the have-nots of these same opportunities. Consequently, social justice advocates argue that the government has the moral obligation to rectify that injustice. Yet that so-called "injustice" is not logically valid because most advanced societies have labor laws that protect the worker against any potential exploitation from the employer.[51] Thus, the worker is neither arbitrarily deprived of having access to wealth nor opportunities because he/she is already earning a wage that could be multiplied in different investments if the latter decides to invest. By using government to equalize access to resources, wealth, and opportunities; social justice has hindered society on the economic and social aspects.

The Economic Impediment of Social Justice

In America, social justice has become the new resort to alleviate economic inequalities between people and social classes. The current trend of social justice in the United States underlines the misleading premise that the top one percent controls all the wealth while the bottom 99 percent who produces that wealth, does not have access

---

[50] *What is Social Justice?* Pachamama Alliance (2019).
[51] Novak, Michael. "Social Justice: Not What You Think It Is." *Heritage Lectures.* No. 1138. The Heritage Foundation. (2009).

to it. Moreover, this fallacious premise accentuates the fact that most millionaires and billionaires have inherited the wealth that they have today from their predecessors. This assessment is clearly erroneous.

According to a 2017 survey from Fidelity Investments, 88 percent of millionaires in America are self-made.[52] Only 12 percent inherited significant money, and most did not grow up in exclusive country club neighborhoods. It suggests that 88 percent of those self-made millionaires started within the bottom 99 percent then worked their way up by climbing the social ladder. Yet social justice proponents argue that the wealthy are the ones who have deprived those of lower social classes of not having access to wealth and capital. To fix that "injustice"; a progressive income tax has been imposed at the national level and in most states.[53]

If it is morally right for the government to redistribute the wealth in order to ensure that everyone has the same access to that wealth, is it then morally right for the government to arbitrarily deprive those who have access to wealth and resources, of their good fortune and give it to those who do not have it on the mere basis that they simply do not have it? It is important to understand that "the state can only give to Peter what it takes away from Paul" because the state is intrinsically propertied-less. Accordingly, it is fundamentally wrong and morally bankrupt for the state to deprive an individual of his property without his consent. It uses its coercive power

---

[52] Sightings, Tom. "7 Myths About Millionaires." *U.S. News.* (2018)
[53] Blunden, G. H. "A Progressive Income Tax." *The Economic Journal.* Vol. 5, No. 20. (1895). pp. 527-531

through means of punitive taxation to legitimize that deprivation under the guise of "social justice." Moreover, the following data show how states with a progressive income tax system are less productive than states with no progressive income tax.

U.S. States GDP Growth, 2006-2016

─◆─ states with progressive income tax
─○─ states without progressive income tax

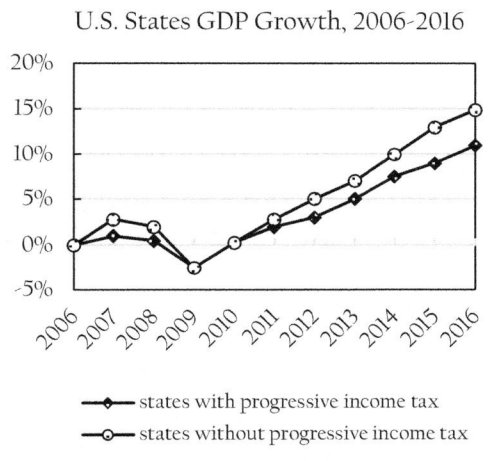

Figure 2.0. Source: Bureau of Economic Analysis

The fundamental conundrum with the progressive income tax is that it is a punitive tax system in which the wealthy are resented for their good fortunes. They are compelled to pay more taxes than everyone else because they generate more wealth than the rest of society. And the goal for making the wealthy pay more than anybody else is for the state to use these taxes to create public assistance programs; programs that underdeliver because its resources are mismanaged by bureaucrats.

Those social welfare programs, however, do not benefit the disenfranchised; but keep them instead in a state of perpetual poverty because the welfare state impedes human capital. The welfare state impedes the development of human capital because it creates a system of dependency.[54] This system of dependency reduces the incentives for the welfare recipients to leave the welfare state and to become economically autonomous. For example, the number of food stamps recipients increased from 26 million recipients in 2007 to 48 million recipients in 2013 as we can see in figure 2.1.

Growth of Food Stamps Recipients, 2007-2016

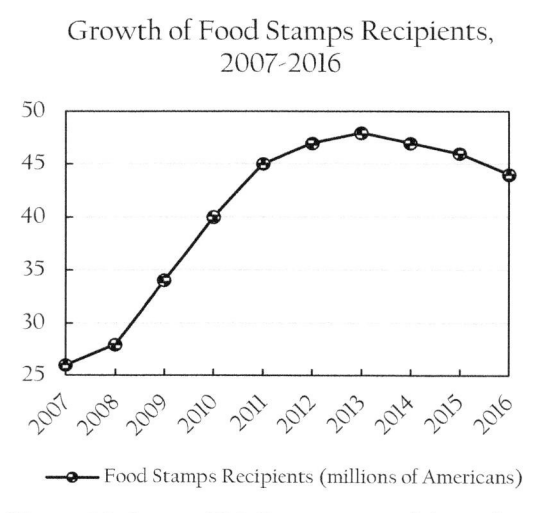

Figure 2.1. Source: U.S. Department of Agriculture

---

[54] Spalding, Matthew. "Why the U.S. has a Culture of Dependency." *Political Op-Ed.* Cable News Network. (2012).

The Social Impediment of Social Justice

The social impediment of social justice principally focuses on access to opportunities and the reduction of unfair privileges. Proponents of social justice argue that the government has the moral obligation to ensure that all members of society have access to the same opportunities, whether it is access to education, access to healthcare, or access to housing. This means that it is the role of government to create a system in which the marginalized members of society would have access to those social goods. Although the intention is irrefutably genuine, it has not produced good outcomes. The truth of the matter is that social justice has undermined meritocracy.

Undeniably, higher academic institutions such as the University of Pennsylvania, Harvard University, or Stanford University; have adopted an affirmative action policy, which is a government-mandated policy enforced in the 1960s whereby a school's admission policy based its decision to accept a student into the program, not on objective metrics such as test scores, or grade point average, but criteria such as race, ethnicity, gender, and sexual orientation; in other words, any criterion that does not objectively demonstrate the intellectual value of the student.

Such a method did create an impediment to the social advancement of those who objectively deserve to be in certain schools.[55] For example, Harvard University was sued in 2018 by several students of Asian background, who have accused the Harvard admission committee of

---

[55] "Affirmative Action" *Legal Information Institute.* Cornell Law School

purposefully discriminating against them on the basis that a great part of the student body at Harvard is occupied by Asian students, and that students of Hispanic and Black American background do not have that accessibility to attend schools like Harvard.[56] By trying to provide greater access to Hispanic and Black American prospective students, Harvard did discriminate against Asian applicants who applied for the same program.[57]

The data show that amid all racial groups of students who have applied at Harvard University between 1995 to 2013, Asian American students have scored higher SAT scores than their White, Hispanic, and Black American peers.[58] Asian-Americans scored 767 across all sections, while Whites scored 745 across all sections, Hispanic-Americans scored 718 and African Americans score 712. By discriminating against Asians, Harvard University did undermine the meritocratic system in education.

---

[56] Verbruggen, Robert. "Two Points about the Harvard Affirmative-Action Ruling." *National Review.* (2019)

[57] Verbruggen, 2019

[58] Avi-Yonah, Shera; McCafferty, Molly C. "Asian-American Harvard Admits Earned Highest Average SAT Score of Any Racial Group From 1995 to 2013." *The Harvard Crimson.* (2018)

Average SAT Score for Admitted
Students to Harvard by Race

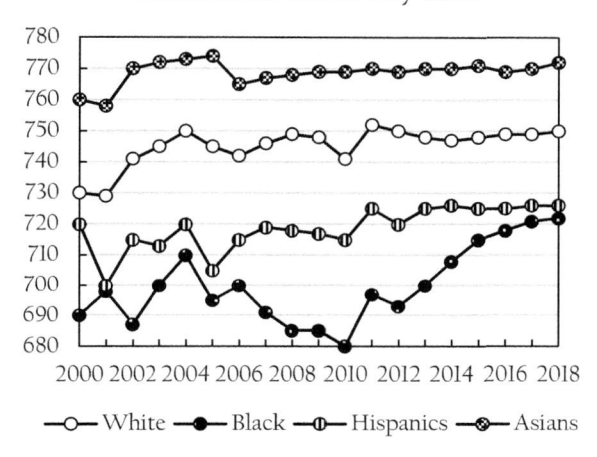

Figure 2.2. Source: Court Documents Submitted by Harvard University

It does not mean that some students attending these universities are not privileged, they indeed are. But by utilizing affirmative action, the selection upon which a student's acceptance is determined does a disservice to the students who come from underrepresented communities because they are selected; not based on the intellectual value that they would bring to the program but on the basis of their skin color and ethnic background. Such a process mismatches their academic skillset with the academic standards of the school they attend.[59] For example, at the University of Texas, the typical Black student receiving a race preference was

---

[59] Perry, Mark, J. "The Downside of Affirmative Action: Academic Mismatch." *American Enterprise Institute.* (2012)

placed at the 52nd percentile of the SAT; the typical White was at the 89th percentile.[60] In other words, the University of Texas put Black American students who scored in the middle of the college-aspiring population amid highly competitive students.[61] Nonetheless, it does not mean that every Black student is incompetent to attend highly selective schools. It is factually true that some Black students have excelled in these schools. But using the concept of social justice to equalize access to opportunities and reduce privileges in the educational system did not favor those that it intended to help.

Summary on Social Justice

Social justice, in all its attempts, seeks to create a more egalitarian society wherein people could have equal access to all sorts of things, did create more inequalities which result in making the disenfranchised lagging even more. Social justice, despite its well-intended premises, impedes economic and social advancement.

3. Minority Groups' Success: Evidence from Asians and Indian Americans

Institutional racism has been said to be the cause of generational poverty for minority groups in the United States. However, if this statement was entirely true, then Asian Americans (Chinese, Japanese, Taiwanese, Korean, and Filipino descents) and Indian Americans (Indians, Bangladeshi, & Sri Lankan descents) would have been poor for generations the same way the Black community

---

[60] Sander, Richard; Taylor, Stuart. "The Painful Truth about Affirmative Action." *The Atlantic.* (2012)
[61] Sander & Taylor, 2012.

has been. However, there is an overwhelming amount of evidence that utterly disproves the claim that institutional racism is the reason why minority groups are poor.

The existence of racism cannot be denied in American society. It has existed and still exists. But how much of a role it now plays in the advancement of minority groups, especially of Black Americans? Are there discriminatory laws today in this twenty-first century that inhibit Black Americans from advancing as was the case back in the days of Jim Crow? Is White privilege still the reason why generational poverty is perpetuating its way in the Black community?

There is no discriminatory law today, at any level of government (local government, state government, & federal government) in this twenty-first century, which prevents an individual or a family from a minority ethnic group from prospering socioeconomically in the United States. Asian Americans and Indian Americans are perhaps the two most prominent ethnic minorities who are the most socioeconomically advanced. Like Black Americans, these two groups have not been exempted from persecution and racial discrimination.

a) *Racism against Asian Americans*

Asian Americans have long been considered as a threat to a nation that promoted a White-only immigration policy.[62] They were called a "yellow peril": unclean and

---

[62] De Leon, Adrian. *The Long History of Racism Against Asian Americans in the U.S.* PBS. (2020)

unfit for citizenship in America.[63] In the nineteenth century, White Americans spread xenophobic propaganda about Chinese uncleanliness in San Francisco, which fueled the passage of the infamous Chinese Exclusion Act, the first law in the United States that barred immigration solely based on race.[64] By 1885, following the Chinese Exclusion Act, a large number of young Japanese laborers, together with smaller numbers of Koreans and Indians, began arriving on the West Coast where they replaced the Chinese as cheap labor in building railroads, farming, and fishing.[65] Growing anti-Japanese legislation and violence soon followed and in 1907, Japanese immigration was restricted by a "Gentleman's Agreement" between the United States and Japan.[66] On February 19, 1942, President Franklin Delano Roosevelt signed Executive Order 9066 to incarcerate people under suspicion as enemies to inland internment camps.[67] While the order also affected German- and Italian-Americans on the East Coast, the vast majority of those incarcerated in 1942 were of Japanese descent.[68]

Asian Americans are seen as submissive: culturally prone to be physically unaggressive, politically docile, and accommodating.[69] In part, this stereotype arises from

---

[63] De Leon, 2020
[64] De Leon, 2020
[65] *Asian Americans Then and Now*, Center for Global Education. Asia Society.
[66] Ibid.
[67] De Leon, 2020
[68] De Leon, 2020
[69] Harvard Law Review Association. "Racial Violence Against Asian Americans." *Harvard Law Review*. Vol. 106, No. 8. (1993), pp. 1926-1943

average physiological differences in weight and height between Asian Americans and other members of other racial groups.[70] In part, it stems from Western interpretations of certain Asian cultural and aesthetic values.[71] Furthermore, Asian Americans are regarded as the *model minority*, succeeding by virtue of a pious work ethic.[72] As a minority, Asian Americans rest beneath Whites in the social hierarchy, but as the model minority, they stand above other racial minorities.[73]

b) Racism against Indian Americans

Indian Americans are the second-largest immigrant group in the United States.[74] They have also encountered racial discrimination. Indeed, both U.S. and foreign-born Indian Americans report significant discrimination based on skin color—35 percent and 27 percent, respectively.[75] Interestingly, U.S. born-Indians report twice as much discrimination along with gender and religious lines than those born outside of the United States.[76]

The following data (figure 2.3) present the experience of Indians with discrimination, by place of birth. The heightened levels of discrimination that U.S.-born Indian

---

[70] Ibid. p. 1931
[71] Ibid. p. 1931
[72] Ibid. p. 1931
[73] Ibid. p. 1931
[74] Badrinathan, Sumitra; Kapur, Devesh; Kay, Jonathan; Vaishnav, Milan. "Summary." *Social Realities of Indian Americans: Results from the 2020 Indian American Attitudes Survey.* (2020). Carnegie Endowment for International Peace. pp. 1-63
[75] Ibid. p. 43
[76] Ibid. p. 43

respondents reported compared to immigrants hold true across categories—whether skin color, gender, religion, or even caste.[77] U.S.-born Indian Americans overwhelmingly blame non-Indians when it comes to discrimination on the basis of country of origin or skin color.[78]

Experience with Discrimination, by Birth Place

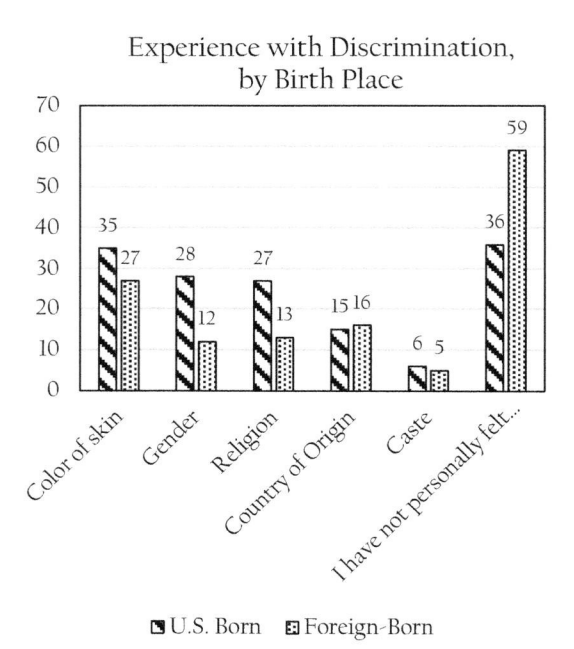

Category	U.S. Born	Foreign-Born
Color of skin	35	27
Gender	28	12
Religion	27	13
Country of Origin	15	16
Caste	6	5
I have not personally felt...	36	59

Figure 2.3. Source: 2020 Indian American Attitudes Survey

---

[77] Ibid. p. 43
[78] Ibid. p. 44

c) Asian American Socioeconomic Success

Despite the racism and all the discrimination that Asian- and Indian Americans have endured, how have they succeeded socioeconomically in avoiding generational poverty while Black Americans remain in this situation?

Asian-and Indian Americans highly value intellectual activities over any other type of human activity. Indeed, the most striking success of Asian Americans and Indian Americans is in educational attainment.[79] While 36 percent of Whites, 23 percent of Blacks, and 16 percent of Hispanics have a bachelor's degree or more, 54 percent of Asians do as we can see in figure 2.4.[80]

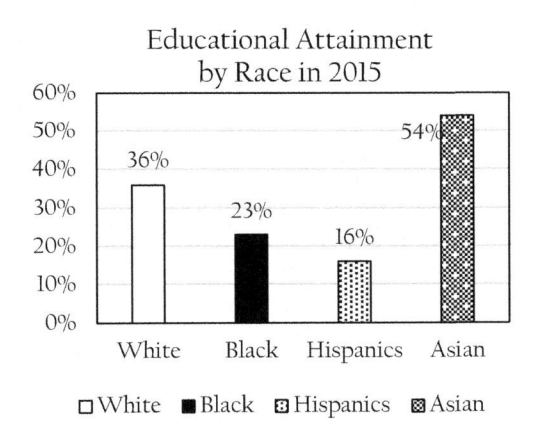

Educational Attainment by Race in 2015

- White: 36%
- Black: 23%
- Hispanics: 16%
- Asian: 54%

---

[79] Joo, Nathan; Reeves, Richard V.; Rodrigue, Edward. "Asian-American Success and the Pitfalls of Generalization." *Brookings Institute.* (2016).

[80] Ryan, Camille L.; Bauman, Kurt. "Educational Attainment in the United States: 2015." *Current Population Reports.* U.S. Department of Commerce—Economics and Statistics Administration. U.S. Census Bureau.

Figure 2.4. Source: U.S. Department of Commerce &
U.S. Census Bureau

Furthermore, while 14 percent of Whites have advanced degrees, 21 percent of Asian Americans do.[81] David Brooks, in his New York Times article entitled *The Learning Virtues*, argued that culture is the fundamental factor that explains the socioeconomic success of Asian Americans. He pointed to a Chinese attitude toward education that aims to "perfect the learning virtues in order to become, ultimately, a sage, which is equally a moral and intellectual state."[82] These virtues include sincerity, diligence, perseverance, concentration, and respect for teachers.[83] But education is not the original engine of the socioeconomic success of Asian Americans. Their belief in hard work is perhaps more vital than their belief in education.

As a matter of fact, it is their belief in hard work that they transcend into education. Education is more of a means to an end for Asian Americans rather than an end in itself. It is the means through which hard work is mostly expressed. In a College Board/National Journal survey of 1,272 adults ages 18 and older, the majority of members of all ethnic and racial minorities agreed with the statement "young people today need a four-year college degree in order to be successful."[84] However, Asian Americans are more likely to believe that academic achievement results from greater effort, rather than

---

[81] *Brookings Institute*, 2016

[82] *Brookings Institute*, 2016

[83] *Brookings Institute*, 2016

[84] *Brookings Institute*, 2016

greater skill.[85] And this belief is backed by superior academic outcomes for Asian Americans.[86] There is undeniably a correlation between the academic achievements of Asian Americans and their level of income. When we look at the data released by the U.S. Census Bureau in figure 2.5., we see that the Asian American community utterly dominates other racial groups including Whites. In 2020, an Asian American household made $94,903.00, Whites made $74, 912.00, Hispanics made $55,321.00, and Blacks made $45, 870.00.

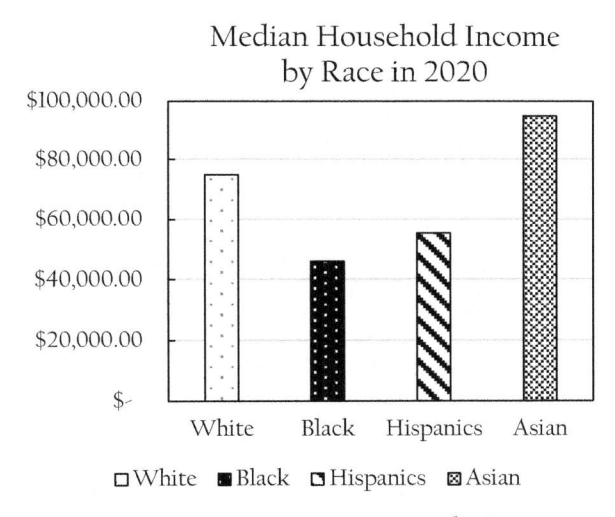

Figure 2.5. Source: U.S. Census Bureau. Note: The Income reported has declined due to the COVID-19 pandemic. The median household income for each racial group was higher in 2019 than in 2020

---

[85] *Brookings Institute*, 2016
[86] *Brookings Institute*, 2016

d) *Indian American Socioeconomic Success*

Indian American success is very much like Asian Americans'. Indian Americans are the wealthiest and most educated immigrants in the United States.[87] The wealth acquired by Indian Americans is not rocket science according to Indian economist, Nirvikar Singh, who wrote *The Other One Percent: Indians in America.* According to Professor Singh, the success of Indian Americans is based on the selection process in India, which has favored the most privileged members of society—those from the educated, upper classes—and U.S. immigration policies further advantaged high-achieving students and skilled workers.[88] Dr. Singh emphasized that the simplest policy prescription was to emphasize that all Indians coming to America would have access to education.[89]

The massive flow of Indians to the United States coincides with the time when the U.S. government relaxed its immigration policies after 1965.[90] Coming disproportionately from the upper castes, those early migrants sought educational and employment opportunities that set in motion a pattern of success that would be replicated across generations.[91] 68 percent of India-born immigrants living in the United States have

---

[87] McNulty, Jennifer. "Success of Indians in the U.S. showcases Importance of Education." *Newscenter.* (2017). University of California, Santa Cruz
[88] McNulty, 2017
[89] McNulty, 2017
[90] McNulty, 2017
[91] McNulty, 2017

college degrees; Indian immigrants concentrated in industries like information technology; their average incomes are generally higher than the average incomes associated with their level of educational attainment (like Asian Americans); and their rates of self-employment and entrepreneurship are higher at both the high and lows ends of the income scale, reflecting engagement in both hospitality and retail, as well as medicine and the high-tech industry.[92] The following data present the median annual household income among Indians in the United States compared to all Asians in the United States.

Median Household Income between Indians and Asians Living in the United States in 2019

- All Asians in the U.S.
- All Indians in the U.S.
- US-born Indians
- Foreign-born Indians

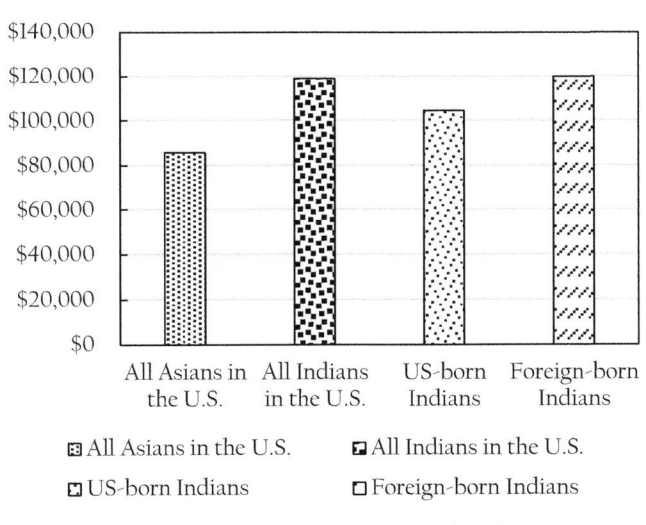

Figure 2.6. Source: Pew Research Center

---

[92] McNulty, 2017

The data show us that Indian Americans, whether U.S.-born or foreign-born, are socioeconomically more successful than all Asian Americans combined (Chinese, Korean, Japanese, Filipinos...etc.) while Asian Americans already earn more than most White Americans, and within Indian Americans, foreign-born Indian Americans earn even more than U.S.-born Indian Americans.

4. Summary

The evidence overwhelmingly suggests that racism is no longer the factor in preventing minority groups from achieving socioeconomic success in American society, and the Asian and Indian American communities are a mere reflection of that. All minority groups, at some point in the history of this country, have suffered from racism and discrimination. Yet, Asian and Indian Americans have overcome these obstacles by changing their attitudes. They amplified the need to invest in education, as the main means to avoid generational poverty.

More importantly, the evidence suggests that no racial and ethnic group is deterministic. If Asian and Indian Americans were able to become socioeconomically successful, it is because they chose to do so, they chose to reassess their collective behavior and make the changes that ought to be made in order to achieve positive outcomes. The changes made demonstrate a consequentialist attitude toward responsibility and collective outcomes.

Individually, most Black Americans are financially improving, and are better-off than a decade or two ago.

But collectively, the Black community is economically lagging compared to other racial minority groups. The substantial difference between the Black community and Asian and Indian American communities is that the latter has developed and ensconced an economic powerbase while the former lacks this very economic powerbase they need to avoid generational poverty.

Asian and Indian Americans have heavily invested in their human and social capital to strengthen their economic powerbase. They fathomed that if their powerbase was well-established, meaning having the resources and infrastructures to create generational wealth perpetually within the community, this generational wealth will enable their community to sustain itself much longer and to even influence the impact of laws and regulations on society. On the other hand, the Black community has a very strong political powerbase, the strongest of all minority groups, but has never diligently invested in its economic powerbase, which is investing in its human capital to create the infrastructures they need to in order to circumvent the perpetuity of generational poverty.

3. BLACK CULTURE & THE WELFARE STATE

Among all the communities living in the United States, the Black community is the community that mostly lags in terms of material and financial resources to achieve collective emancipation. The enactment of the Civil Rights Act of 1964, on the one hand, has enabled the Black community to exercise its right to vote. It has elevated Black Americans from being treated as second-class citizens to legitimate, and lawful citizens of the United States. It empowered Black Americans to cherish their political liberties. On the other hand, the Civil Rights Act of 1964 warranted the government to play a much more intrusive and interventionist role in the Black community, which led to unintended yet harmful consequences.

1. Political and Economic Rights of the Black Community After the Civil Rights Act of 1964

The obtainment of political rights has subverted the economic rights for Blacks through the enforcement of the welfare state. The welfare state has worsened the economic condition of the Black community. From its inception, the implementation of the welfare state was done with the most genuine intentions. Its purpose was to ensure that individuals would not live cashless. It was to ensure that individuals would have at the very least access to the most basic needs. The welfare state, however, turned out to be a trap where Black Americans are kept into a system of perpetual poverty and permanent victimization.

Welfare state policies have, in fact, dismantled the Black family structure. The economic milieu in which the War on Poverty arose is noteworthy. Between 1950 and 1965, the proportion of people whose earnings put them below the poverty level has decreased by more than 30 percent.[93] The Black poverty rate, in particular, had been cut nearly in half between 1940 and 1960, and in various skilled trades during the 1936-59 period, the incomes of Blacks relative to those of Whites had more than doubled.[94]

From 1965 to 1969, government-provided benefits increased by a factor of 8; by 1974 such benefits were an astounding twenty times higher than they had been in 1965—moreover, federal spending on social-welfare programs amounted to 16 percent of America's Gross National Product (GNP), a far cry from 8 percent figure of 1960.[95] By 1977 the number of people receiving public assistance had more than doubled since 1960.[96] The following data show how means-tested welfare programs

---

[93] Perazzo, John, "How The Liberal Welfare Destroyed Black America: What Democrat Voters And Political Leaders Refuse To Believe", *FrontPage Magazine*. (2016).
[94] Perazzo, Ibid.
[95] Perazzo, Ibid.
[96] Perazzo, Ibid.

have substantially grown since the 1950s as a percentage of gross domestic product over the past half-century.[97]

Means-Tested Welfare or Aid to the Poor

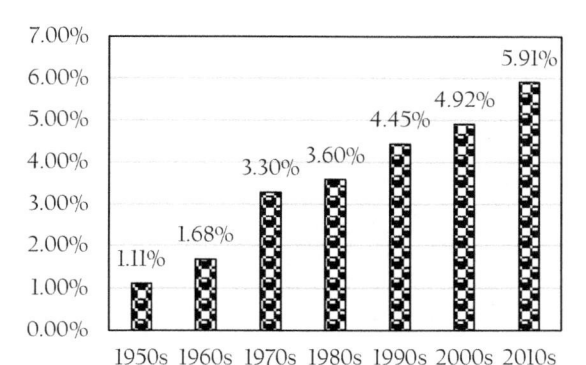

Decade	Average percentage of GDP during Decade
1950s	1.11%
1960s	1.68%
1970s	3.30%
1980s	3.60%
1990s	4.45%
2000s	4.92%
2010s	5.91%

Figure 3.0. Source: The Heritage Foundation

2. The Dismantlement of the Black Nuclear Family

The most devastating by-product of the welfare state was the corrosive effect it had on the Black community.[98] As provisions in welfare laws offered ever-increasing economic incentives for shunning marriage and avoiding the formation of two-parent families, illegitimacy rates rose dramatically.[99] As a matter of fact, means-tested welfare programs such as food stamps, public housing,

---

[97] Rector, Robert; Menon, Vijay. "Understanding the Hidden $1.1 Trillion Welfare System and How to Reform It." *Backgrounder*. No. 3294. (2018). The Heritage Foundation.
[98] Perazzo, Ibid.
[99] Perazzo, Ibid.

Medicaid, daycare, and Temporary Assistance to Needy Families—penalized marriage in the Black community.[100] Indeed, a mother generally received far more money from welfare if she was single rather than married. Once she has a husband, her benefits are instantly and substantially reduced by roughly 10 to 20 percent.[101]

Welfare programs for the poor incentivize the very behaviors that are most likely to perpetuate poverty.[102] The marriage penalties that are embedded in welfare programs can be particularly severe if a woman on public assistance weds a man who is employed in a low-paying job.[103] The results of welfare policies discouraging marriage and family were dramatic for the Black community.

In the mid-1960s, the out-of-wedlock birthrate was scarcely 3 percent for Whites, 7.7 percent for Americans overall, and 24.5 percent among Blacks—by 1976, those figures had risen to nearly 10 percent for whites, 24.7 percent for all Americans as a whole, and 50.3 percent for Blacks.[104] and today, the numbers stand at 29 percent for Whites, 41 percent for the nation overall, and 73 percent for Blacks.[105]

---

[100] Perazzo, Ibid.
[101] Perazzo, Ibid.
[102] Perazzo, Ibid.
[103] Perazzo, Ibid.
[104] Perazzo, Ibid.
[105] Perazzo, Ibid.

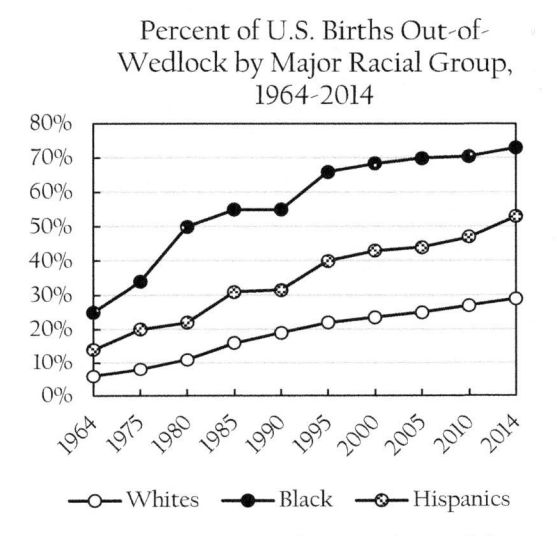

Percent of U.S. Births Out-of-Wedlock by Major Racial Group, 1964-2014

—○— Whites   —●— Black   —⊗— Hispanics

Figure 3.1. Source: U.S. National Center for Health Statistics

Children in single-parent households are burdened not only with economic, but also profound social and psychological disadvantages. For example, Black youngsters raised by single parents, as compared to those who grow up in intact married homes are likely to be physically abused; to display emotional disorders; use drugs; perform poorly in school; to be suspended or expelled from school, to drop out of high school; to behave aggressively, and even violently; to be arrested for a juvenile crime; to serve jail time before age 30, and to go on to experience poverty as adults.[106]

The lack of paternal authority and emotional stability within the Black family structure is the main factor that

---

[106] Perazzo, *Ibid.*

determined the upsurge of crime rate among Blacks. Despite the well-intentioned programs of the welfare state, it has engendered more damages to the Black family than it has helped it.

3. Welfare State and Unemployment in the Black Community

The policies of the welfare state did not only deconstruct and dismantle the Black family structure, they have also subsequently incremented Black unemployment. In every census from 1890 to 1954, Blacks were either just as active as or more so than Whites in the labor market.[107]

Prior to the welfare state policies like the minimum wage laws, Black Americans improved their living standards through enormous productive gains—an impressive feat, given the lawless injustice of the Jim Crow laws. Unfortunately, these well-intentioned policies have widened the racial gap.[108] This can be seen with the following data which illustrate the wealth gap across the major racial groups.

---

[107] Williams, Walter E., "The Welfare State's Legacy", *Creators Syndicate*. 2007

[108] Philipps, Grants, "US History Shows the Minimum Wage Has Harmed the Black Community", *Panam Post.* (2016)

Median Family Wealth by Race, 1992-2016

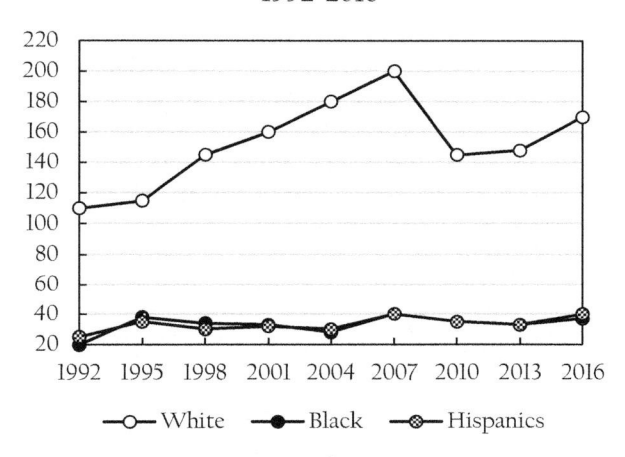

Figure 3.2. Source: 2016 Survey of Consumer Finances & Federal Reserve Board. Note: The Unit of measurement in these data is expressed in thousands of dollars. For example, 20 = $20,000.

The turn of the twentieth century was marked with reduced foreign labor from immigration restrictions and increased demand for American goods—the North's industrial economy boomed and attracted Blacks away from the South's agriculture industry, largely due to recruitment efforts by Northern industrialists.[109] Blacks migrating north assimilated into the workforce by accepting lower wages in return for work experience. This pay gap was surely not ideal, but it allowed the average Black migrant to experience a 30 percent increase in annual earnings by moving north.[110] Ultimately, Blacks

---

[109] Phillips, Ibid.
[110] Philipps, Ibid.

achieved huge gains in wages, education, and political expression, despite the social injustices of the time.

Furthermore, the Black labor force developed considerably and, by 1940, the Black-White wage gap had sharply declined.[111] Black employment began to be negatively affected in 1938 when Congress legislated the Fair Labors Standards Act (FLSA) and instituted the first minimum wage of $0.25 per hour.[112] The essence of the minimum wage law is that it makes it illegal for an employer to hire a low-skilled individual. The law prohibited Black youths from entering the labor market, harming their long-run employment potential.[113]

According to the Employment Policies Institute (EPI), 16- to 24-year-old males without a high school diploma are the most affected by the minimum wage law. Indeed, the EPI found that every 10 percent increase in a federal or state minimum wage decreased Black youth employment by 6.5 percent.[114]

In 1956, a 33 percent increase in the minimum wage precipitated an alarming turnaround for Blacks, and by 1960, unemployment for young Black males had nearly doubled to 22.7 percent while increasing only slightly for

---

[111] Philipps, Ibid.
[112] Philipps, Ibid.
[113] Philipps, Ibid.
[114] William, E. Even, David A. Macpherson, "Unequal Harm: Racial Disparities Consequences of Minimum Wage Increases", *Employment Policies Institute.* (2011) Policy Research.

young Whites.[115] The reason the minimum wage does not benefit minorities, especially Blacks, is because, in a labor market, employers face a real cost if they discriminate against minority workers; they pay more for labor than their non-discriminating competition.[116]

The administration of the minimum wage laws created an artificially high wage that all employers have to pay, which has the effect of removing that economic pressure to not discriminate and actually enables a racially biased employer to let racial considerations drive hiring decisions.[117]

As of today, the federal government wants to promulgate the minimum wage to $15.00 per hour in the 2020s. It entails that whatever unemployment that would be created by a higher minimum wage, it will be concentrated among young and untrained, and even those who are ill-favored by the current arrangements.[118] If Congress passes a new minimum wage law that makes it illegal for employers to pay less than $9.00 per hour, and for workers to accept less than that amount, it will further an erosion of the market for unskilled workers, especially Black teens.[119]

---

[115] Garthwaite, Craig, "Minimum Increase Hurts Low-Income Families", *Employment Policies Institute.* (2005)
[116] Poper, Rob, "High Minimum Wages Were Designed to Hurt Minorities", *Ethan Allen Institute.* (2018)
[117] Poper, Ibid.
[118] Poper, Ibid.
[119] Poper, Ibid.

Effect of Hypothetical Implementation of a $9.00 Minimum Wage on Black Teenagers

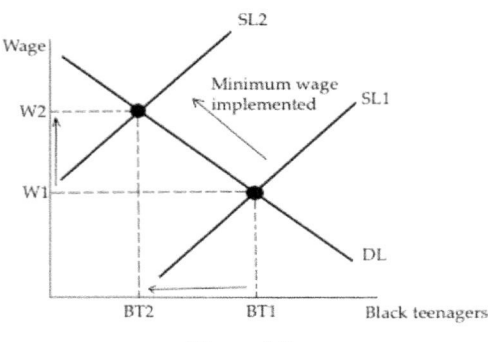

Figure 3.3

The welfare state, which was supposed to facilitate access to employment for Blacks, has instead substantially hardened their conditions for obtaining employment in the labor market. That is, surplus labor resulting from minimum wage laws makes it cheaper to discriminate against minority workers than it would be in a market economy, where there is no chronic excess supply of labor.[120]

Passing up qualified minority workers in a market economy means having to hire more other workers to take the jobs they were denied, and that in turn usually means whether having to raise the pay to attract the additional workers or lower the job qualifications at the existing pay level—both of which amount to the same thing

---

[120] Perry, Mark, "Thomas Sowell on the differential impact of the minimum wage." *American Enterprise Institute.* (2016)

economically, higher labor costs for getting a given amount of work done.[121]

4. The Impact of the Welfare State on Economic Inequalities

Welfare state policies, which have prompted the dismantling of the Black family structure, as well as the implementation of the minimum wage laws—have also invigorated more economic inequalities within the Black community.

Furthermore, the welfare state has stimulated more crimes within the community. Studies have shown that children from single-parent families are more likely to become involved in criminal activity—nearly 70 percent of juveniles in state reform institutions come from fatherless households, as do 43 percent of prison inmates.[122] As a practical matter, the welfare culture tells the man he is not a necessary part of the family, and the role of the young Black man is supplanted by the welfare check.[123]

At the social level, the Black male reflects the domestic authority in the family. The Black man as the domestic authority of the house is the guide, the reference, and the path on which the members of the family rely. By dispossessing him of his manhood, the welfare state has emasculated the Black man. It has annihilated his authority and has indeed destroyed his self-esteem

---

[121] Perry, Ibid.
[122] Tanner, Michael D., "Relationship Between The Welfare State and Crime." *Cato Institute.* (1995)
[123] Tanner, Ibid.

because it has made him dependent on its [welfare] system. Being dependent understandably signifies the loss of autonomy. By making the Black man an individual dependent on public assistance, the welfare state has certainly deprived him of all his responsibilities which determine his authority.

Moreover, when the Black man becomes dependent on public assistance, he subsequently becomes a social waste, a useless element of society that does not contribute to human capital nor to the production of wealth. The goals of the welfare state were not initially to dismantle the Black community, but then in its quest to expand its administrative power over the masses, and particularly over Blacks; the government has used the welfare state to implement policies that have produced outcomes which have led to economic, political, and social stagnation within the Black community. The government has continuously used the welfare state to keep the poorest under its control. Blacks may have the right to vote, and other forms of political rights, but their dependence on the welfare state proves that they are still maintained as second-class citizens in American society.

The worst of all is that the Black community has always been conditioned by the fact that having a Black individual as a political figure or holding an important political office will bring them economic salvation. For example, most of the Black community thought that President Obama, as being the first Black individual to have become President of the United States, would improve their living conditions. They believed that President Obama would bring them the economic liberation and independence they had been waiting for, for ages. Obviously, this expectation has been misleading for the Black community. To illustrate this point, there are two factors upon which the Obama administration held back economic progress for Blacks: a lack of jobs in inner cities and poor educational opportunities.[124] Under the Bush administration, Black unemployment was at 9.7 percent, and under the Obama administration, this number became double-digit and rose to 15.6 percent[125] before it eventually dropped to its natural rate later during his second term.

Lastly, the educational policies of the Obama administration have reduced most school choice programs for Blacks. Obama's educational policies limited the choice for Blacks to choose the adequate education they wanted for their children, which made the government decide for them what is better for their children.

It is not because a politician belongs to a certain community that he is necessarily the providential man who will bring salvation to his community. And it was the case with President Obama. Salvation is, in fact, a personal feature of the human condition that strictly belongs to the individual himself. And the reason why salvation is a personal feature of the human condition is because human beings are stimulated by their own self-interest, which is a completely natural element and the

---

[124] Moore, Stephen, "Why Trump is better for Black America than Obama ever was." *The Hill.* (2017)
[125] Mitchell, Daniel J. "Obama's Failure on Jobs: Four Damning Charts." *Forbes.* (2011)

phenomenon of any civilized society. For economic salvation to be the quintessential factor of emancipation for the Black community, it is first and foremost important to reconstruct the Black family structure. Adjunctively, economic prosperity can only be within the Black community if each member of the community pursues his own interest because the pursuit of one's self-interest involuntarily contributes to the economic growth of society.

Furthermore, each member of the Black community should maximize his skills and abilities to produce wealth. As previously noted, the accentuation of talent and skills of everyone stimulates human capital as well as the production of wealth because everyone concentrates on the task where he performs the best.

Black people are no less intelligent nor less skillful than Whites, Hispanics, Asians, Indians, or Arabs. What they need to do is simply not to rely on government means-tested programs, but to rely on obtaining a good education in order to acquire the necessary skills that would strengthen their potential and would make them more competitive in the labor market. So long as one depends on government assistance, he or she will remain economically unproductive and stagnated. That is the law of welfare dependency.

4. BLACK CULTURE & COUNTERPRODUCTIVE HABITS

This chapter is perhaps the most crucial chapter of this entire book because it is the one that determines and elaborates the central idea of our hypothesis. The central idea of our hypothesis maintains that the scourge of generational poverty that plagues the Black community is not due to racism or the legacy of slavery but to the counterproductive behaviors that the Black community has adopted as a culture.

In the second chapter entitled "Racism and Generational Poverty in the Black Community," the evidence we presented, suggested that racism has very little to do with the current socioeconomic condition of the Black community. We demonstrate how minority groups such as the Asian and Indian American communities have overcome the burden of racial discrimination to now become the most socioeconomically advanced racial groups of all minorities.

In order to elaborate our hypothesis, it is preponderant to define what Black culture is. Without a concrete definition of "Black culture," it is impossible to rigorously develop the link between Black culture and the counterproductive habits we decry.

1. An Analysis of Black Culture

This book is entitled *Black Culture & Generational Poverty*. Indeed, the title of this book suggests that the understanding of Black culture is crucial in order to fathom the social correlation established between the Black community and generational poverty. Black culture is an evolving culture.

The culture of a community generally accommodates itself to the different periods of its history. Black American culture had two phases: the pre-civil rights phase and the post-civil rights phase. We maintain that the evolution of Black culture from the pre-civil rights era to the post-civil rights era has been a harmful evolution, a regression rather than a progression.

a) Black Culture in the Pre-Civil Rights Era

The pre-civil rights era is the period from the abolition of slavery in 1865 to the formalization of the Civil Rights Act of 1964 in 1964. This is ninety-nine years of culture for the Black community. During those ninety-nine years, Black culture was a conservative culture that promoted the values of the nuclear family, work ethic, and self-sufficiency.

This period was a painful time for the Black community because racial segregation in southern states and discriminatory laws in the northern and midwestern states prevented Black people to be socioeconomically emancipated. Yet it was during these periods of racial tensions that the Black community developed tremendous resilience.

In order to be socioeconomically emancipated, the Black community practiced the concept of respectability politics. The term "respectability politics" was first used in the context of Black women and their efforts to distance themselves from the stereotypical and disrespected aspects of their communities.[126] In other words, respectability politics refers to the way that people attempting to make social changes would present their demands in a way that is acceptable to the dominant standards in their society.[127] The concept of respectability politics was primarily promulgated by Booker T. Washington.

Booker T. Washington reasoned that the politics of respectability was the best approach for the Black community to become self-sufficient because the system in which they lived was a White-established system, with laws and customs based on the standards of Western life.[128] In such a system where Blacks lacked having the economic, financial, and political resources to adequately fight the White-established system, attempting to fit in these standards was the best course of action to ensure that Black Americans would also have a place in American society.

---

[126] Paisley, Harris. "Gatekeeping and Remaking: The Politics of Respectability in African American Women's History and Black Feminism." *Journal of Women's History.* Vol.15. (2003) p. 213

[127] Nuñez-Franklin, Brianna. Democracy Limited: The Politics of Respectability. *Democracy Limited: The Suffrage "Prison Special" Tour of 1919.*

[128] Young, Jeremy C. "Booker T. Washington and the White Fear of Black Charisma." *Black Perspectives.* (2017)

Booker T. Washington understood very well that in heterogeneous societies such as the United States, where different cultures and racial groups coexist, this coexistence only takes place when the dominated racial groups respect the standards of the dominant racial group. To respect the standards of the dominant group did not mean rejecting one's own cultural standards. On the contrary, Washington saw an opportunity for Blacks to take advantage of this situation by using these standards to maximize their skills and ameliorate their work ethic in order to even be better than Whites at their own crafts. Therefore Booker T. Washington was quite adamant about the need for Black people to invest in their education.

Booker T. Washington saw education as the pillar of a community's success. His vision of education was not strictly limited to the context of academia. Education to him meant the perpetual continuation of learning. This perpetual continuation of learning was to him industrial education. Industrial education, one historian has observed, meant for Washington "training in industriousness."[129] Washington accepted the common nineteenth-century attitudes that through self-help, one could rise from poverty to riches.[130]

The growth of industrial education in Black schools reached its zenith during the years 1880-1915.[131] Various

---

[129] Booker T. Gardner, "The Educational Contributions of Booker T. Washington." *Journal of the Negro Education.* Vol. 44, No. 4. (1975). pp. 502-518
[130] Ibid. p. 506
[131] Ibid. p. 506

societies established industrial schools where trades were taught to develop economic independence and self-support.[132] Black communities supported their schools in many ways.[133] They taxed themselves heavily, donated money, materials, and labor in the construction of numerous schools.[134] They also gave more than two million dollars during the ten-year period 1895 to 1905 to higher education as well as to the support of their neighborhood schools.[135] The following data show how the rate of illiteracy of the Black community significantly decreased from 1870 to 1960. This decrease is thanks to the insistence of Booker Washington on education.

Rate of Illiteracy of the Black Community, 1870-1960

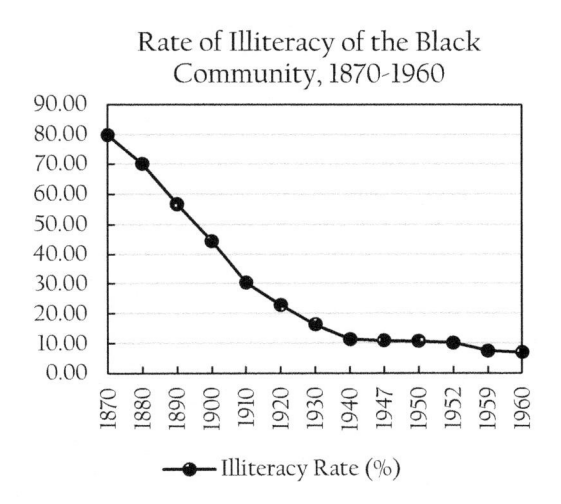

Figure 4.0. Source: U.S. Department of Commerce,

---

[132] Ibid. p. 506
[133] Ibid. p. 507
[134] Ibid. p. 507
[135] Ibid. p. 507

Bureau of the Census, Historical Statistics of the United States, Colonial Times to 1970

The adoption of respectability politics allowed Blacks to increase their employment rates. Although the unemployment rate was consistently higher for Blacks than Whites, the rate of participation of Blacks in the labor force did not go unnoticed between 1940 and 1952.

As a matter of fact, an interesting change in the labor market occurred. More Blacks shifted from agriculture to the service industry. In 1940, 33.1 percent of the agricultural labor force was Black. In 1952, only 20.1 percent of the agricultural labor force was Black. This dramatic decline of Blacks in the agricultural labor may be related to the fact that more Blacks began to become more literate. In order to verify if our assumption is true, we statistically tested the impact of the illiteracy rate on agricultural employment for Blacks. The results of our regression are displayed in figure 4.1.[136]

---

[136] We used a linear regression to test correlation between the illiteracy rate of Blacks and their rate of employment in the agricultural sector. The model is the following: (**Agriculture** = β_0 + β_1 **IlliteracyRate** + ε) We used the data from the U.S. Department of Commerce, U.S. Census Bureau and the Historical Statistics of the United States. (n=18). The data was designed by decades until the year 1940 when it was spread every three or four years on average.

Impact of Black Illiteracy Rate on
Black Employment in the Agricultural
Sector, 1870-1964

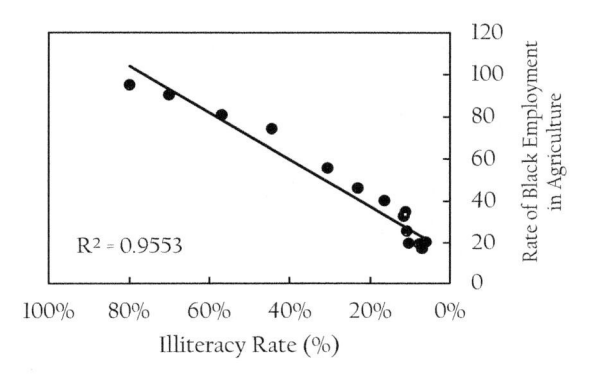

$R^2 = 0.9553$

Figure 4.1. Source: Author's calculations

The evidence suggests that there is a strong correlation between Black illiteracy rate and their employment rate in the agricultural sector. Indeed, as more Blacks knew how to read, write and count, they also began to veer toward jobs that require less physical effort, and pay slightly more. Furthermore, the geographical distribution of Blacks employment also changed, because 90 percent of all Black agricultural workers in 1940 were in the South.[137] It is interesting to observe that moving away from the agricultural sector was a way for Blacks to no longer be seen as mere uneducated peasants and to better integrate themselves into American society by getting involved in more sophisticated trade jobs that require more technical skills and knowledge.

---

[137] Bedell, Mary S. "Employment and Income of Negro Workers—1940-52." *Bureau of Labor Statistics.*

During the pre-civil rights period, the Black nuclear family was intact, and the abortion rate was relatively low as well as the rate of children born out of wedlock compared to the post-civil rights period. The use of respectability politics, as much as it may have been unpleasant at times, has tremendously helped the Black community to have access to economic opportunities despite the repressive era in which they were living. In trying to live up to the standards of White Americans, Black Americans had fostered a better education for their children and inculcated them the values that would allow them to be successful in life and move upward the social ladder.

b) *Black Culture in the Post-Civil Rights Era*

As was argued in the previous chapter, the welfare state is mostly responsible for negatively impacting Black culture. There is no need to explain again in-depth the impact of welfare policies on the Black community since that was covered in the precedent chapter. It is essential to say that the post-civil rights period (1964-present) has been a period of cultural and social regression where the Black community abandoned its conservative values to adopt liberal values, which are, however, not compatible with Black culture.

The cultural and social regression of the Black community after the enforcement of the Civil Rights Act was effectuated by the abandonment and rejection of respectability politics for the embracement of "hood" culture. The politics of respectability allowed Black Americans to integrate more easily into American society and to climb the steps of social mobility. The Black community rejected the politics of respectability without having any leverage to compete on an equal footing with Western culture. The trap is that the Black community thought that political power was the leverage that would allow them to compete adequately with the customs of Western culture. Though, political power has never allowed any community on earth, whatever its race, to emancipate itself socioeconomically. For a community to emancipate itself socioeconomically, it is imperative for it to have a solid economic foundation because it is the economic foundation of a society that determines its political system. Not the other way around.

The American political system was built under the customs of Western culture, especially that of British culture and customs. The laws and regulations that govern the nation are all based on the moral codes of British culture. Therefore, when a politician gains political power, s/he is obliged to exercise that power within the framework of Western customs. And President Obama is the perfect example of this, as we illustrated it in the previous chapter on the welfare state. President Obama did not exercise the power granted to him by the Constitution to strictly focus on the economic and social issues of the Black community, not because he did not want to but because he could not. He exercised his power within the framework of Western customs that the Constitution assigned him. Another example that is worth being mentioned is that of Nelson Mandela. Many Black South Africans thought that once Mandela became president, he would solve their problems. The result has been the same as that of President Obama. The South African political system is also designed within the framework of Western customs (Afrikaner's customs); hence President Mandela could not do much. Although Black South Africa gained political power, they remained socioeconomically poor. Consequently, in hoping that a Black American would gain political power and use that power to alleviate their problems, the Black community misunderstood that this Black American politician (whoever that may be) would have to exercise his power within the framework of Western norms because it is these norms that determine the mechanisms of the political system whether at the local, state, or federal level. If American society were determined by the customs of Black culture, then the political system would operate according to the codes of Black culture.

It is important to emphasize that the social regression being discussed does not mean that all Black Americans have culturally regressed. On the contrary, many Blacks have become socioeconomically self-sufficient by maintaining the values of respectability politics, but this self-sufficiency is assessed at the individual level, i.e. how each Black American is doing socioeconomically. In 1940, when the U.S. Census Bureau started asking about educational attainment, only 7 percent of Blacks had a high school education compared with 24 percent for the nation as a whole.[138] In recent years, Black educational attainment has been much closer to the national average, and today, 88 percent of Blacks have a high school diploma.[139] So, individually, Blacks are progressing. The

---

[138] Cheeseman Day, Jennifer. "88% of Blacks Have High School Diploma, 26 % a Bachelor's Degree." *U.S. Census Bureau.* (2020).
[139] Cheeseman Day, 2020

social regression being decried focuses on the collective behavior of community as a whole, compared with other racial minority groups.

While other racial minorities such as Indian and Asian Americans have adjusted their culture to Western standards by maintaining the politics of respectability, the Black community has moved away from it by embracing the virtues of hood culture. The problem is that hood culture has no virtue. It is a destructive culture that is completely antagonistic to the principles of life that lead to self-sufficiency and human dignity. The adoption of hood culture is the reason why poverty has dramatically increased in the Black community to the point of making it generational. Black Americans who entered politics to reduce poverty in the Black community failed because they could not contain the spread of hood culture within the community.

Black political leaders, instead of preaching the politics of respectability to facilitate the integration and upward social mobility of Black America, would rather use the politics of resentment to ascertain their own power and maintain their fellow Blacks more resentful and yet poorer than other minority groups. From a political perspective, tapping on the resentment of a minority group that is economically lagging presents a valuable opportunity for its political leader to exert substantial control over their collective behavior.

As Dr. Sowell noted in his pathbreaking book *Wealth, Poverty and Politics*, originally published in 2015, but revised and enlarged in 2016, there are four principles that political leaders of lagging minority groups apply to ensure their control over their people. First, these leaders avow the assurance that the lags of their people are not their fault.[140] They inculcate in their people's minds, the deterministic belief that they are responsible in no way for their own socioeconomic condition. Second, these leaders give the assurance that the lags of their people are the fault of the most fortunate groups that they already envy and resent.[141] Third, these leaders assure their people that their culture is as good as anybody else's, if not better.[142] Fourth, These leaders assure their people that what they need and deserve is a demographically defined "fair share" of the economic and other benefits of society, sometimes supplemented with some kind of reparations for the past injustices or some special reward for being indigenous "sons of the soil."

In addition, racial and ethnic leaders have every incentive to promote the isolation of the groups they lead—despite the fact that isolation has been a major factor in the poverty and backwardness of many different peoples around the world.[143] If political leaders of the Black community such as Maxine Waters or Al Sharpton encourage their members to adopt a consequentialist attitude rather than a deterministic one, then they will no longer have power and influence within the community because their people will soon realize that they did not need them to become self-sufficient since the steps to

---

[140] Sowell, Thomas. "Politics and Diversity." *Wealth, Poverty, and Politics.* (2016). p. 269. Basic Books. ISBN: 978-0465096763
[141] Ibid. p. 269
[142] Ibid. p. 269
[143] Ibid. p. 269

achieve self-sufficiency are essentially embodied in the personal choices we make daily.

2. Hood Culture and Its Counterproductive Habits

Hood culture is a culture that advocates for lawlessness. It is an unhealthy culture that encourages treachery, promiscuity, dishonesty, violence, disrespect for authority, and the rejection of education and hard work. This culture of inequity has been detrimental to the Black community, especially since the welfare state has been enforced in the 1960s through the War on Poverty policies.

Dr. Sowell argued that the hood culture that is now the dominant culture in urban Black neighborhoods originates with White English immigrants who settled in the South and had an aversion to work, were prone to violence, neglected education, were sexually promiscuous, lacked entrepreneurial acumen, were improvident, enjoyed lively music and dance, were given to drunkenness and engaged in religious oratory that was strident, emotional, and flamboyant.[144] These practices, which formerly were those of the Whites of the lower social classes, have been adopted by the Blacks of these same social classes. Indeed, hood culture is essentially practiced in low-income neighborhoods. Some members of the Black community claim pride in these counterproductive practices because, for them, these practices define the authenticity of Black culture.

---

[144] Harris, Robert J. "Essay Review: On Thomas and African American Life and Culture." *The Journal of African American History.* Vol. 91. No. 3. (2006), pp. 328-334

Ironically, there is nothing authentic about practices that keep someone perpetually poor.

a) The Problem with Hip-Hop Culture

Hip-hop culture is today the bedrock of hood culture. This culture promotes violence in the streets, the use of drugs, abundant sexual promiscuousness, and living a flashy and lavish lifestyle. These counterproductive habits praised in hood culture are done with pride and are seen as the path to achieving wealth.

A hip-hop artist like Blac Youngsta is rather lionized by members of the Black community than a man like Clarence Thomas would. Though Clarence Thomas is a Supreme Court Justice who earned his law degree from Yale Law School (one of the best law schools in the world and arguably the number one law school in the United States), which is perhaps one of the greatest achievements a Black person in America could ever hope for (based on the racial history of this country), a man like Blac Youngsta is rather highly praised by members of the Black community for his music, and influence. However, the themes and lyrics of his music incentivize violence, sexual promiscuity, and death. Many young Black teenagers look up to him as well as many other rappers as a symbol of success. Why is Blac Youngsta more successful than Clarence Thomas in the Black community although Clarence Thomas reflects a much more genuine and cleaner approach to success?

Indeed, many Black teenagers are convinced that becoming a hip-hop artist today is the best and surest path out of poverty. According to ZipRecruiter's data, the majority of hip-hop artists earn between $34,000 (25th percentile) to $61,000 (75th percentile) a year with top earners (90th percentile) making $83,000 or more annually across the United States while the national average earning for a hip-hop artist is $54,584 a year or $26 per hour.[145]

Hip-Hop Artist Salary

	Annual Salary	Month Pay	Weekly Pay	Hourly Wage
Top Earners	$83,000	$6,916	$1,596	$40
75th Percentile	$61,000	$5,083	$1,173	$29
Average	$54,584	$4,548	$1,049	$26
25th Percentile	$34,000	$2,833	$653	$16

Table 4.0. Source: ZipRecruiter's Data

By analyzing these figures, one can see that the average annual salary of a hip-hop artist is significantly lower than the average annual national income per capita, which is $67,521 according to the Bureau of Labor Statistics. Hip-hop artists, on average, earn $12,937 less than the national average income. The evidence suggests then that going the hip-hop route does not guarantee a safe way to get out of poverty. According to the United States Courts data on compensation, a federal judge earns, at least, about $200,000 a year. A federal judge

---

[145] *ZipRecruiter Data*, (2022)

would earn an average salary of $239,475.[146] As we can see in figure 4.2., a District Judge earns $223,400 a year, a Circuit Judge earns $236,900, an Associate Justice earns $274,200 and the Chief Justice of the Supreme Court earns $286,700. Evidently, not everyone can become a federal judge. Becoming a federal judge requires seven years of post-secondary education (4 years of undergraduate, 3 years of legal education, and passing the bar exam), about a decade or so of legal experience as a practicing attorney, and a lot of political connections. By comparing the occupation of a judge to a hip-hop artist, we can see that the job of a judge is much more rewarding than that of a hip-hop artist as a federal judge earns nearly five times more than an average hip-hop artist. Yet being a hip-hop artist is more admired and celebrated by the Black community than being a judge.

Judicial Compensation in 2022

☐ Federal Judges Salary

---

[146] Judicial average salary was calculated based on how much each federal judgeship makes annually.

Figure 4.2. United States Courts

The essence of this ostensible paradox is based on the desire for instant gratification. Hood culture resents education as the surest path to success in life because it is long, lonesome, and produces no exaltation. People who do not value intellectual prowess do not find any amazement or exaltation in academic accomplishments. Being a hip-hop artist, on the other hand, is a prideful accomplishment in hood culture because hip-hop culture depicts strength and assertion. Hip-hop artists, in their lyrics, usually boast themselves for having done prison because being in prison shows that they have endured pain and overcame it, and this survival of the pain they endured in prison has made them even stronger. Hence, there is an exaltation from that kind of experience. Hood culture is a culture that craves admiration and instant gratification.

However, the reality is far crueler than what hip-hop artists would have us believe. Having done prison is not an accomplishment that one shall be proud of because having been in prison is a serious social handicap for the former inmate. Someone with a prison sentence on his record is unlikely to be trusted by members of society. Such a person will never be able to rent an apartment, take a loan from a bank, or even be hired. Having been in jail is the surest path to generational poverty.

Moreover, not all hip-hop artists become and remain multi-millionaires. Many successful hip-hop artists have gone poverty-stricken because, despite all the money and wealth they accumulated, they mismanaged that wealth, spent it on things they did not need, and as a result, they wasted all that wealth into debts that they could not repay. Hence, hip-hop culture does not set the right example that Black teenagers should follow. Instead, it unconsciously promotes generational poverty because hood culture is a culture that has been passed along for many decades, and those who practice such a culture have been poor for many generations.

b) *Sexual Promiscuity*

Sexual promiscuity is a cardinal characteristic of hood culture. It is, undeniably, one of the most devastating and deadliest features of hood culture. Hood culture is a culture that focuses on hypersexuality.[147] We must emphasize that sexual promiscuity is, conversely, not a special feature of Black culture. It is a vice of human nature that has been practiced in all societies since the dawn of human civilization. On the other hand, as a cultural characteristic, sexual promiscuity is practiced more frequently by individuals from lower social classes, regardless of their skin color. This does not mean that individuals in upper social classes do not practice sexual promiscuity. They do, but they are more discrete about it than low-income people are.

Sexual promiscuity is a phenomenon that persists in hood culture. In such a culture of lawlessness, having many sexual partners and sexual encounters is for Black women who practice hood culture, a way to show their value to men. They use their sex as an asset to show their

---

[147] Hypersexuality is an excessive preoccupation with sexual fantasies, urges or behaviors that is difficult to control.

worth as women to the dominant men of the neighborhood in exchange for security. This is a method for hood women to enhance their hypergamy. For Black men who practice hood culture, sexual promiscuity is a way to assert their manhood and dominance over women.

In hood culture, having sex with as many women as possible shows male virility, strength, and dominance. According to hood-culture standards, a man who has a sexual relationship with only one woman is seen as weak and exhibiting an inability to conquer. Likewise, a woman who only has one sexual partner is perceived as a woman who is unable to attract men. In hood culture, men and women are both devoted to sexual prowess to either be accepted by the community as one of theirs or to ascertain their influence over the community. Thus, sexual promiscuity in hood culture is the barometer to measure influence and power. This attitude is very similar to the animal's kingdom wherein 20 percent of dominant males mate with 80 percent of females. Sexual promiscuity is a natural trend in the animal's world because this is how they perform their mating process. But in human societies, sexual promiscuity is rather an unnecessary process to determining how mating should be done.

Sexual promiscuity is pernicious because it encourages those who practice it to embrace irresponsibility. In low-income neighborhoods where hood culture is the lifestyle, sexual promiscuity incentivizes the birth of children out of wedlock. In addition to the government which subsidizes such behavior through welfare programs, people who practice hood culture through sexual promiscuity are doomed to remain in perpetual poverty because they lack the financial means to provide for their children due to their limited education and the lack of employment opportunities in these neighborhoods. Sexual promiscuity discourages people from marrying while marriage is one of the best pathways to avoid poverty. Indeed, most of those who practice hood culture are unaware of the economic benefits of marriage.

Being married helps couples obtain social security boosts and income tax breaks, it improves their credit scores, enables couples to buy a home, to have quality health insurance, and so on.[148] In short, being married helps couples escape poverty while in hood culture, marriage is perceived as a sign of weakness. Hood culture promotes single-parenthood through sexual promiscuity. The data illustrated in figure 4.3 show that the Black community is the racial group to have the second-highest rate of single-parenthood after Whites, and consequently the minority group to have the highest rate of single-parenthood in the nation. Within those 28 percent of single-parenthood in the Black community, 30 percent of single parents are mothers while only 16 percent are fathers.

---

[148] Schwab-Pomerantz, Carrie. *Does Marriage Bring Financial Benefits?* Charles Schwab. (2020)

Single-Parenthood by Race and Gender in 2018

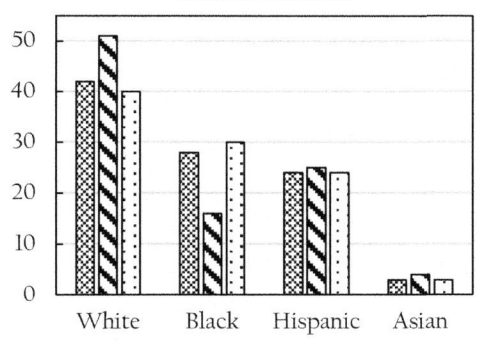

[Bar chart showing percentages for White, Black, Hispanic, and Asian categories with Total, Among Fathers, and Among Mothers bars]

⊠ Total ◩ Among Fathers ▫ Among Mothers

Figure 4.3. Source: Pew Research

Sexual promiscuity in hood culture has been extremely harmful to the Black community because it has increased the rates of rapes, sexual diseases, and children born out of wedlock. According to the Center for Disease Control (CDC), Black Americans account for a higher proportion of people with HIV compared to other races and ethnicities.[149] In 2018, Black Americans account for 13 percent of the national population, but 47 percent of these 13 percent have HIV.[150] And 16.1 percent of Black Americans have died of HIV in 2019, which is the highest rate among racial groups and ethnicities. It is sincerely heartbreaking to see that a corrosive behavior such as sexual promiscuity is sustained, adulated, and incentivized in low-income Black neighborhoods while it

---

[149] *HIV and African American People*, CDC.
[150] Ibid

109

is destroying these neighborhoods and harming the Black community at large.

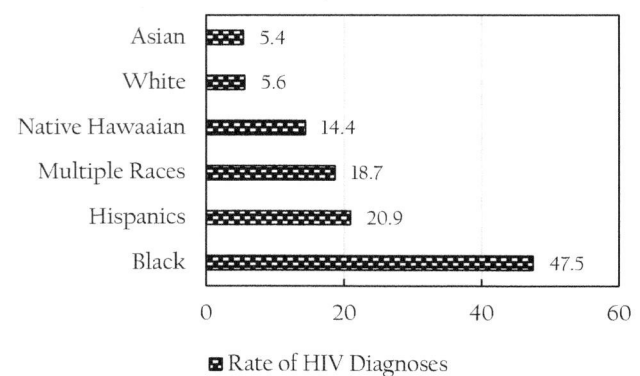

Rates of new HIV Diagnoses per 100,000 by Race in 2018

Race	Rate of HIV Diagnoses
Asian	5.4
White	5.6
Native Hawaiian	14.4
Multiple Races	18.7
Hispanics	20.9
Black	47.5

Figure 4.4. Source: Center for Disease Control

HIV Death Rate in the U.S. in 2019 by Race

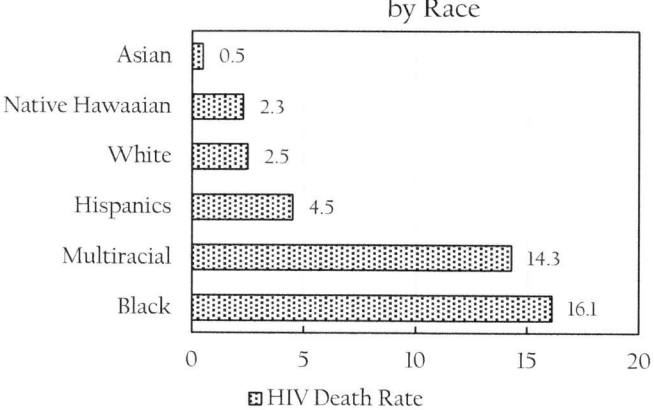

Race	HIV Death Rate
Asian	0.5
Native Hawaiian	2.3
White	2.5
Hispanics	4.5
Multiracial	14.3
Black	16.1

Figure 4.5. Source: Center for Disease Control

c)   Aversion to Work

Work aversion behavior is not a cultural characteristic of the Black community. However, it is a central trait in hood culture. In hood culture, work is perceived as a conundrum or a defect rather than a means of emancipation. The reason for this aversion to work is based on the quest for permanent excitement and exaltation. Since hood culture is geared towards instant gratification, those who practice it give themselves up to all sorts of activities where hard work is neither a necessity nor valuable. Hood culture derives its exultation from excessive alcohol consumption, drugs, and endless social gatherings.

Unlike hood culture that is widely practiced in the Black community, the most productive racial minorities are socioeconomically more advanced than the Black community because they value the virtues of work over those of counterproductive activities. Indeed, productive minority groups see work as the only source of social emancipation. Work is the means through which they would achieve economic, financial, and social freedom. More importantly, work is the means through which they would create generational wealth. It is, therefore, not surprising to see why the Indian and Asian American communities are wealthier than Whites and other racial groups in America. For productive minority groups, excessive alcohol consumption, drug consumption, and endless social gatherings are all habits that set a community backward because it perpetuates laziness, bad behavior, and poverty. They see these activities as counterproductive and a waste of human and social capital.

Again, the conundrum with hood culture is that it is a culture that would rather sacrifice long-term goals and benefits for short-term gratification. Let us develop a hypothetical example. Let us assume that two male teenagers, one Black and the other Asian, both sixteen years old, are given $500 to spend on whatever they want. Let us assume that the Black teenager was raised in hood culture while the Asian teenager was raised in traditional Asian values. When spending those $500, the Black teenager purchased a pair of Jordan's for $350 and spent the remainder on miscellaneous activities while the Asian teenager spent his whole $500 on a data science certificate on Coursera to learn how to program, which should take about a year to complete. Both teenagers are naturally content with their respective purchases. When we observe the attitude of these two teenagers, we realize that from a rational and economic standpoint, the Black teenager made a decision that will not benefit him in the long run. The rationale is that a pair of Jordan's will depreciate in value as soon as this teenager starts wearing it. A pair of shoes, no matter how great the brand may be, is a depreciative asset that only has a short-term utility span. The Black teenager may wear this pair of Jordan for a couple of years then those shoes' quality will begin to fade away. If he decides to sell these shoes, he will have to sell them at a much lower price than the price at which he bought them initially. On the other hand, the Asian teenager made a decision that will benefit him in the long run. In learning how to program, this teenager has invested in an appreciative asset, which is himself.

Programming is a new skill that he will acquire, which will make him competitive in the labor market. By investing in his skills, the Asian teenager has now the guarantee that he will earn a higher salary in the near future as he will be gaining more work experience after completing his college degree. Skills appreciate in value because the more skilled one becomes at something, the more expertise that person gains at that thing. And the labor market invests in individuals who have skills. Skills are intrinsic value because they are within the individual while Jordan's, cars, and any other type of depreciative assets, are extrinsic.

The Black teenager's decision was prompted by the eagerness to be praised by his entourage for owning a pair of Jordan's. The Black teenager believed that it was more valuable for him to own something of value that will elevate his status among his peers for a short period of time rather than investing in something that will take a long time before the results become fruitful. The reason why the Black teenager's first instinct was to buy a pair of Jordan's is that depreciative assets are what the members of his entourage value the most. Thus, he believed that possessing that kind of asset would make him fit into his community. The Asian teenager's decision, on the other hand, was motivated by the desire to not have to suffer in the future. The Asian teenager understood that it was preferable to invest in something that may not pay off immediately but in the long run. Data scientists today earn on average $126,830 according to the Bureau of Labor Statistics, which would place that person in the 75th percentile (top 25 percent of the richest households in America) of the income distribution.

Therefore, the Asian teenager is sure to be earning that kind of income at some point in time in his career because he built the skills required to perform that kind of job. If the Black teenager was not raised into hood culture, his first instinct would have been to spend his $500 on something more lucrative, or on some appreciative assets rather than depreciative assets.

Hood culture resents private initiative and any form of attitude that embraces the virtues of hard work. Hood culture considered the virtues of work as being "White," meaning that only White people are the type of people who find enjoyment in working. So, any racial group that promotes the virtues of hard work is considered to be acting "White." The same goes for believing in science, which is another aspect of life that hood culture considers "White."

Hood culture perceives science as an activity solely associated with White culture. Therefore, a person who believes in science and the use of the scientific method is considered to be acting "White." But what hood culture fails to realize is that science is not a characteristic solely attached to White culture. It is a feature attached to any culture that seeks economic development. It is remotely impossible for a community to develop economically without the use of the scientific method because the scientific method is the one that allows the construction of infrastructures as well as the transformation of raw resources into alternative uses. The scientific method has existed since the birth of Christ. All the civilizations that have achieved whether regional, continental, or world dominance, have done so by using the scientific method.[151] What has changed over time was the method of inquiry in the scientific method. As time evolved, human societies began to use more sophisticated tools to apply the scientific method.[152] At some point in time, Egypt, which was then a Black civilization, was the most advanced civilization on the planet. This socioeconomic advancement was mainly due to Egypt's reliance on the scientific method.[153] For example, Egyptian medical textbooks such as the Edwin Smith Papyrus (c.1600 BCE) apply the following methods: examination, diagnosis, treatment, and prognosis to the treatment of disease, which displays strong parallels to the basic empirical method of science.[154] Egyptian medicine was the most advanced in the world at that time, and Greek philosophers and mathematicians even came to Egypt to receive their scientific training.[155] This illustration shows us that Black people were not foreign to the scientific method. On the contrary, they were one of the first civilizations to use this method extensively, which enabled them to achieve world dominance at some point in the history of human civilization. Rejecting science as a cultural feature does not work in the favor of the Black

---

[151] Achinstein, Peter. "General Introduction." *Science Rules: A Historical Introduction to Scientific Methods.* John Hopkins University Press. (2004). ISBN: 0-8018-7943-4

[152] Gauch, Hugh G. *Scientific Method in Practice.* Cambridge University Press. (2003). p. 45. ISBN: 978-0-521-01708-4

[153] Lloyd, G.E.R. "The Development of Empirical Research," *Magic, Reason and Experience: Studies in the Origin and Development of Greek Science.*

[154] Ibid.

[155] Sallam, Hassan. "Aristotle, Godfather of Evidence-Based Medicine." *Facts, Views & Vision in ObGyn.* Vol. 2, No. 1 (2010). pp. 11-19

community, especially hood culture. A community or culture that rejects the scientific method as part of its customs is doomed to remain in poverty for a very long time.

3. Summary

Hood culture is a culture that operates on emotion rather than reason. When we analyze the reasons that motivate those who practice this culture, we realize that these reasons are purely based on pathos rather than logos. Hood culture is fueled by the zeal for instant gratification. Instant gratification is like a drug. In hood culture, instant gratification is endlessly pursued in order to produce the same superficial elevating effects that a drug may have on its users: a feeling of invincibility, entitlement, and exaltation. Else, its absence produces a feeling of emptiness, depression, and communal rejection.

It is inconceivable in hood culture to even think about something that will have to produce long-term results. The psychology of hood culture is focused on the "present," "now," "tomorrow does not matter," and "the future is irrelevant." Everything done, based on hood standards, must be done for the gratification of today. Thinking and anticipating the future molds the behavior of the present. When someone knows that he has more to gain in the future than he does now, he would subsequently adjust his behavior according to the goal determined in the future. Hood culture is not concerned with the future. It is a culture where "planning for the future" has no place to be. It is a culture that acts on instinct and only values the current moment rather than any futuristic event.

The problem with instant gratification is that one has to pay a very high price to benefit from an effect that is certainly exhilarating but ephemeral. In other words, the predicament with instant gratification is that its cost exceeds its value. All the pathological behaviors that hood culture promotes are counterproductive behaviors that pursue endless elation. These behaviors promoted by hood culture are behaviors that lead to poverty, prison, diseases, and death. Generational poverty is entrenched in hood culture, and hood culture is the real scourge that holds the Black community back.

Lastly, we ought to asseverate that hood culture is not intrinsic to Black culture. It is, however, intrinsic to poverty. Hood culture is the cultural identity of poverty. As we saw earlier in this chapter, hood culture was first practiced by poor White English immigrants who move to the South during the nineteenth century. Hood culture is the culture used by lower social classes no matter where they are around the world. It is the culture of resentment, instant gratification, violence, sexual promiscuity, work aversion, and lawlessness. Hood culture is interchangeably perceived as Black culture because it has now become the dominant culture in Black neighborhoods. Black people embrace it as if it was their culture of origin although it is not. Hood culture is not an ethnic culture like the media try to make it seem. It is, in fact, the culture of poverty. Any lower social class, regardless of race and ethnicity, that has embraced such a culture has remained in poverty longer than envisioned. Hood culture does not elevate, it downgrades and kills.

5. BLACK CULTURE, THE VICTIMHOOD MENTALITY & CRITICAL RACE THEORY

The victimhood mentality has become commonplace in American political culture and Western culture in general. In the literal sense of the word, the victimhood mentality consists of a state of mind whereby an individual feels helpless because he has undergone a repressive treatment which has left him a traumatic experience. In American political culture, the victimhood mentality consists of decrying that a social group is socioeconomically backward because it has suffered the damages of an oppressive system imposed on it. The victimhood mentality basically focuses on justifying the reasons that led to the collective trauma of a social group.

In American political culture, the victimhood mentality is most practiced by the Black community. The Black community justifies its socioeconomic backwardness on racism and the oppressive Jim Crow system that lasted nearly a century. The Black community argues that it was the legacy of slavery and institutional racism that put Black people at a tremendous socioeconomic disadvantage. The belief that institutional racism is the cause of the Black's socioeconomic backwardness is a distorted idea that keeps gaining momentum not just in the Black community but also in other minority groups. As a result, this misleading belief created two important yet harmful concepts in American society: critical race theory, and identity politics.

1. Victimhood and Critical Race Theory

Critical Race Theory, also known as CRT, is a social theory developed by the scholars and activists of the civil rights movement. This theory argues that there is an intersection between race and the law.[156] One of the main ideas of CRT is the concept of intersectionality, a qualitative theoretical framework which describes a way in which different forms of inequality and identity are affected by interconnections of race, class, gender, and disability.[157]

The term intersectionality was first coined by civil-rights lawyer, scholar, and Black feminist activist Kimberlé Williams Crenshaw in 1989. Intersectionality, which is a subset of critical race theory, aimed to demonstrate a multifaced connection between race, gender, and other systems that work together to oppress while allowing privilege.[158]

Crenshaw maintains that the institutional racism that governs our political, economic, and social system, is a system that has been structured to domesticate the Black community and prevent it from emancipating itself. For example, in her 60-page article entitled "Mapping the Margins: Intersectionality, Identity Politics, and Violence

---

[156] Borter, Gabriella. "Explainer: What Critical Race Theory means and Why It's Igniting Debate.?" *Reuters.* (2021).
[157] Gillborn, David. "Intersectionality, Critical Race Theory, and the Primacy of Racism: Race, Class, Gender, and Disability in Education." *Qualitative Inquiry.* Vol. 21, No. 3. (2015). pp. 277-287
[158] Crenshaw, Kimberle. "Mapping the Margins: Intersectionality, Identity Politics, and Violence Against Women of Color." *Stanford Law Review.* Vol. 43. No. 6. (1991). pp. 1241-1299

Against Women of Color" published in the *Stanford Law Review*, Crenshaw used the example of rape to demonstrate how intersectionality works and how it pertains to institutional racism. She argued that the use of rape to legitimize efforts to control and domesticate the Black community was well established and that the casting of all Black men as potential threats to the sanctity of White womanhood was a familiar construct that antiracists confronted and attempted to dispel over a century ago.[159]

Critical Race Theory promulgates the belief that an individual's socioeconomic success is directly correlated to their skin color. Thus, according to this theory, since the United States is a society where institutional racism is well-ensconced, social groups that have been marginalized for years, such as Blacks, Hispanics, or women of color, have practically very low chances of succeeding. The advocates of critical race theory further promote the need for the theory to be taught in schools, especially in elementary and middle-school levels.

It is quintessential to reiterate once again that there is no social correlation between someone's skin color and his ability to succeed in life. A person's ability to succeed in life is never based on his skin color but on the choices he makes. The problem with critical race theory is that it blames one social group as being responsible for preventing another social group from succeeding socioeconomically. This theory tells the little Black boy or girl that s/he cannot succeed in life while growing up

---

[159] Ibid. p. 1266

because the little White boy or girl has taken their opportunity to make it in life. This is unequivocally untrue. A Black boy or Black girl is doomed to fail if, and only if, they embrace the virtues of hood culture and its counterproductive behaviors. A Black boy or girl who grows up in a two-parent household, who is raised with the virtues of hard work, self-sufficiency, and personal responsibility, and goes all the way to college to obtain a bachelor's degree, will not fail in life. On the contrary. This Black boy or Black girl will have already accomplished more than needed to avoid generational poverty. A Black person's ability to succeed is not constrained by a White person's "privilege."

Critical Race Theory seeks to blame today's White people for the evils that their ancestors may have inflicted on Blacks and other minority groups in the past. But the problem lies in the fact there is no correlation between the wrong caused by eighteenth-century White people and those of today. The majority of White people living in the United States today come from the waves of migration in the nineteenth and twentieth centuries. These migratory waves coming from Europe were not necessarily linked to the Whites who were already here in America when the United States was becoming a constitutional republic. Once again, the success of Indian and Asian American communities was not constrained by the so-called White privilege. If White privilege were truly effective at preventing minorities from flourishing as CRT advocates would claim, then absolutely no racial minority group would be socioeconomically successful. Critical Race Theory encourages minority groups to embrace victimhood and a defeatist mentality. Such a mentality fuels resentment of others for being successful.

From an economic standpoint, critical race theory increases social costs. CRT is, for example, more concerned with protecting criminals from punishments than with protecting society from crime.[160] The models underlying CRT's policy prescriptions are characterized by assumptions about racial actors and racial markets.[161] Consequently, these proposals endorse governmental regulation of the market and argue against free-market mechanisms to ameliorate social problems.[162]

The political effect of CRT is preferential treatment and social welfare programs for people of color—particularly Black people.[163] The following model shows that when government regulations are enforced to monitor market mechanisms, the social cost increases while the production of wealth decreases.

Impact of Social Cost on Wealth Production

---

[160] Carbado, Devon W.; Gulati, Mitu. "The Law and Economics of Critical Race Theory." *The Yale Law Journal.* Vol. 112, No. 7. (2003). pp. 1757-1828
[161] Ibid. p. 1758
[162] Ibid. p. 1758
[163] Ibid. p. 1758

Figure 5.0.

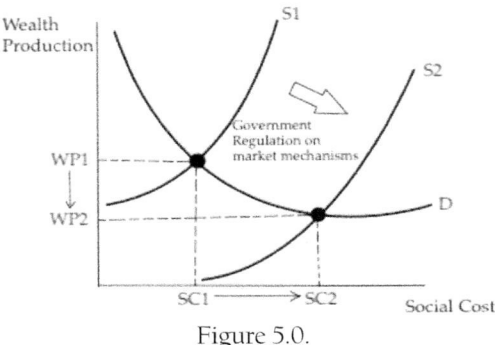

While CRT articulates its conception of race as a social construction at the macro level, focusing primarily on legal and sociopolitical processes,[164] it has not paid attention to the interpersonal ways in which race is produced.[165] That is, CRT often ignores the racial productivity of the choices people of color make about how to present themselves as racialized persons.[166] Government regulations enforced to equate wealth based on race is fallacious because it subsidizes people of color to rely on more government initiatives rather than organizing themselves to create growth. Social programs do increase social cost while subsidizing the victimhood mentality.

Those who adhere to the victimhood mentality argue that these social programs will help them equalize economic opportunities. In reality, these social programs only reinforce their belief to be the victims of a so-called

---

[164] Ibid. p. 1760
[165] Ibid. p. 1760
[166] Ibid. p. 1760

oppressive system. It, therefore, incentivizes them to abandon all types of initiatives to change their life condition since they have already accepted that they are victims, and consequently feel entitled that society owes them back an apology for being members of an oppressed group. This fallacious belief that racism is the cause of the woes of the Black community can be seen when in a survey conducted by the Pew Research Center in 2019 (figure 5.1), 84 percent of Blacks responded that racial discrimination was the main reason why they cannot get ahead while only 42 percent of them acknowledged that family instability was the cause. It should have been the other way around.

In our modern society, Black Americans have access to all possible opportunities to elevate themselves in society. Barack Obama is the first Black president this country has ever had; Clarence Thomas, who was born and raised in poverty, managed to become a Supreme Court Justice of the United States; Reginal Lewis, who also had humble beginnings, managed to become the first Black American billionaire in the United States after building a billion-dollar company, TLC Beatrice International Holdings Inc. The list could go on, but the point to stress here is that if these Black men thought that their skin color was the reason why they could not achieve anything in life then they would have indeed accomplished nothing in life. They would have lamented on their misery and looked for a scapegoat to justify why they were lagging. The victimhood mentality is a psychological issue that professes self-pity and the need to be patronized by advanced groups who may see Blacks as inferior for their refusal to take a consequentialist attitude to life.

Assessment on Why It May be Harder for Black people to get ahead

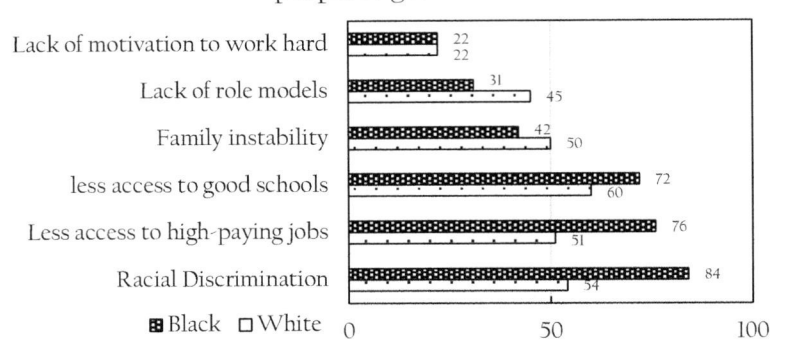

Category	Black	White
Lack of motivation to work hard	22	22
Lack of role models	45	31
Family instability	50	42
less access to good schools	72	60
Less access to high-paying jobs	76	51
Racial Discrimination	84	54

Figure 5.1. Source: Pew Research Center

2. Identity Politics

Identity politics is very much like critical race theory. They sometimes intermingle. But the substantial difference between the two is that identity politics is far more holistic than critical race theory. While critical race theory focuses strictly on the relationship between race and our institutions, identity politics focuses on how race, gender, social backgrounds, and social classes all interact and intertwine with our political, economic, legal, and social institutions.

Identity politics is a sociopolitical ideology that originated from an intent. That intent was to promote equal rights for minorities in order to achieve social inclusion. The predicament with identity politics is that it is grounded in categorizations. It indicates that it separates individuals and places them into different boxes. Based on the different boxes in which the individual is placed, he must therefore align with a certain way of thinking or must accordingly endorse a particular view because his cultural identity and social background may reflect that view. For example, 95 percent of Black Americans voted for President Obama in 2008 and 2012.[167] The reason is simply because Barack Obama was the first Black political candidate, nominated to represent the Democratic Party in the general election of 2008—and having him as president would be a historical moment for the United States and the world—to see that America has elected its first Black President. In 2012, Black Americans massively voted to re-elect Barack Obama in order to keep the status imperturbable. This example illustrates the point that if an individual is Black American, it is spontaneously assumed that he is a Democrat or a liberal.[168]

The most dangerous and vicious aspect of identity politics is that it intertwines personal achievement with cultural identity. It defines the achievement of an individual based on that person's cultural identity. It

---

[167] "How Groups Voted in 2008." *Roper Center for Public Opinion Research.* Cornell University

[168] It is important to stress that the meaning of the word "liberal" has changed. In modern American political culture, a liberal is someone who supports a greater involvement of the government in economic and social affairs. An American liberal believes that it is the role of the government to intervene in the economy when the market fails or to regulate in order to tackle social issues. However, the original meaning of the word "liberal" suggests someone who believed in limited government, economic, political, and social freedom, and the rule of law. Original liberalism is known as *classical liberalism.*

conjectures that the achievements of that individual are not premised on his skills and abilities, but quintessentially on his racial, cultural, religious, and sexual background. Identity politics stresses that the value of an individual is rather measured by his cultural identity than his abilities. In doing so, a person of color would tend to believe that his success is solely due to his external attributes. This has been the case for Kamala Harris when she was elected Vice President of the United States alongside Joe Biden who was elected President in 2020.

When the media praised Kamala Harris for becoming Vice President, they focused on Harris' external attributes such as her gender (first woman Vice President), her race (first Black person to become Vice President), her ethnicity (first person of Jamaican and Indian background to become Vice President) rather than her intellectual abilities, and political experience. Did Kamala Harris qualify to be Vice President of the United States? If so, the objective way to measure her qualifications for the job is to look at her political experience rather than her social background. Looking at her qualifications and political experience, there is no doubt that Kamala Harris qualified for the position of Vice President. She obtained a bachelor's degree in political science from Howard University, a law degree from the University of California Hastings School of Law, she was District Attorney of San Francisco for seven years (2004-2011), Attorney General of California for six years (2011-2017), and a U.S. Senator for four years (2017-2021). Her political experience clearly epitomizes her acumen for the job of Vice President. However, it is preponderant to emphasize that it is not because she qualifies for the job of Vice President that she necessarily deserves to be Vice President. To qualify for the vice presidency and to deserve the vice presidency are not the same thing at all. Kamala Harris may surely qualify for the vice presidency due to her extensive political experience, but her deserving to be Vice President of the United States is not a given.

When Joe Biden was running for the presidency in 2020, he pledged that the vice president will necessarily be a woman, preferably a Black woman, to show his commitment to diversity and inclusion. But if the qualifications to become Vice President were solely limited to these two factors (gender and skin color), then Stacy Abrams was far more qualified than Kamala Harris because she is a woman like Harris and more importantly, she is dark-skinned whereas Harris is light-skinned, and mainly mixed race. Physically speaking, Stacy Abrams looked more authentic than Kamala Harris to fill the position of Vice President as a Black woman. But Abrams was less experienced than Harris politically, and this criterion was what mattered more to Joe Biden than anything else for the role of Vice President since he was Vice President himself under the Obama presidency. Stacy Abrams never held any political office at the federal level. Her highest political office was state representative for the Georgia House of Representatives. Clearly, this is not enough to be considered for the vice presidency. Having federal political experience was a key component to qualify for the vice presidency and Abrams crucially lacked that experience. Even Biden, who is a proponent of diversity and inclusion, fathomed that relying just on external attributes to fit the job of Vice President was not a good metric to make such important choices. A woman of color but with extensive political experience was mandatory to qualify for that position, and Harris perfectly fit the criteria.

Yet the media tried to make Kamala Harris someone who deserves the vice presidency because she is a woman of color. Kamala Harris's skin color and gender are, in no way, correlated with her intellectual abilities and political experience. By focusing specifically on the external characteristics of Kamala as the decisive factors of her qualifications for the vice presidency, the media are trying to convey a message that is however not real.

This message is to say that as long as an individual is a female of non-White skin color, that individual can eventually reach that kind of position in life. Of course, anyone can dream of becoming Vice President. But what the media did not say in their message is that there are a set of prerequisites that ought to be fulfilled in order to be considered for that kind of position, and having an extensive political experience is the most important criterion to have in order to be considered for the vice presidency.

Whether Kamala Harris deserved to be Vice President or not can only be thoroughly assessed in 2024, at the end of the term of Joe Biden. So far, the evidence suggests that Kamala Harris is not performing well as vice president as we can observe in figure 5.2. The data overwhelmingly corroborate our argument that Harris' external attributes do, in no way, impact her ability to perform the vice presidency well. Her disappointing results are based on a number of factors solely linked to her abilities, not her skin color, gender, or ethnicity. It is interesting to see that across genders, more women are unfavorable to her performance as Vice President although she is a woman. Figure 5.3. shows that 48 percent of women are unfavorable to her while only 42 percent of them favor her. And by race, as we can see in figure 5.4, Blacks and Hispanics have a favorable view of her while Whites and other races do not see her favorably. The fact that Blacks mainly, overwhelmingly voted for her as "favorable," shows once again that they prioritize identity politics over her actual and real performances as Vice President.

Favorability Rating of Vice President Kamala Harris in the United States, as of December 2021

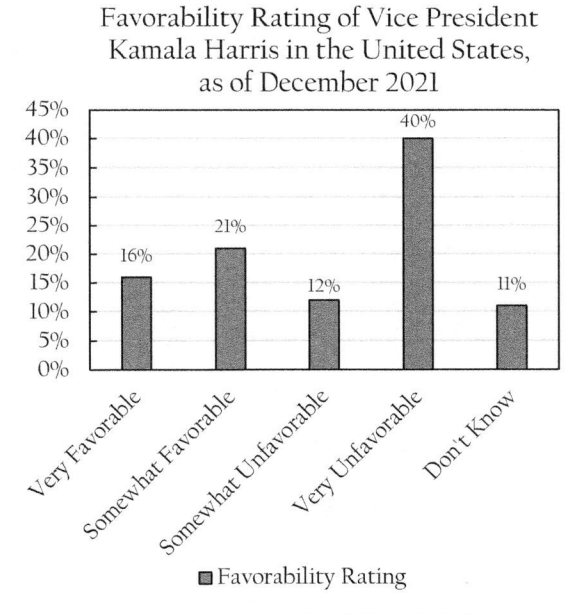

Category	Favorability Rating
Very Favorable	16%
Somewhat Favorable	21%
Somewhat Unfavorable	12%
Very Unfavorable	40%
Don't Know	11%

Figure 5.2. Source: RealClearPolitics

Favorability Rating of Kamala Harris by Gender, as of December 2021

- Women: Favorable 45%, Unfavorable 48%
- Men: Favorable 34%, Unfavorable 62%

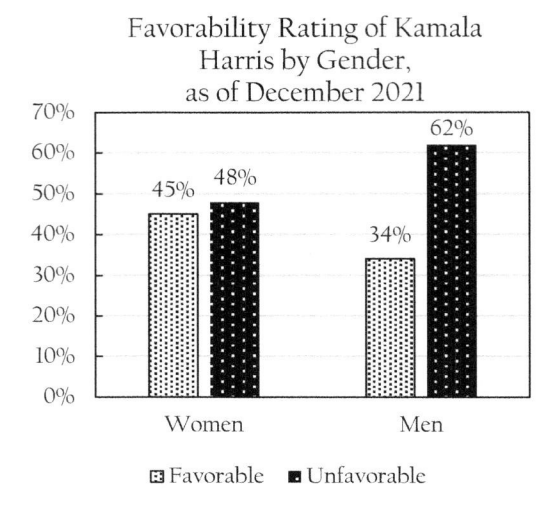

Figure 5.3. Source: RealClearPolitics

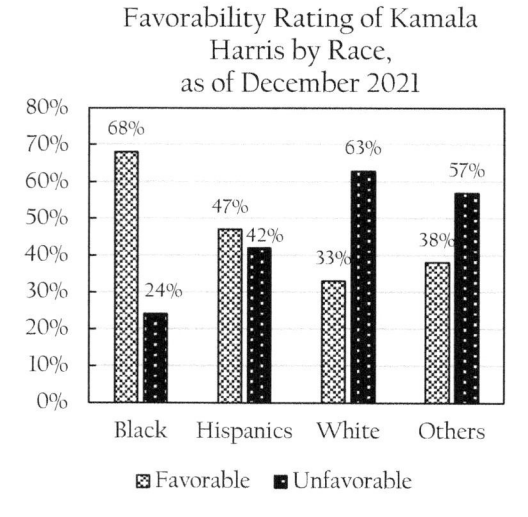

Favorability Rating of Kamala Harris by Race, as of December 2021

- Black: Favorable 68%, Unfavorable 24%
- Hispanics: Favorable 47%, Unfavorable 42%
- White: Favorable 33%, Unfavorable 63%
- Others: Favorable 38%, Unfavorable 57%

Figure 5.4. Source: RealClearPolitics

Kamala Harris may be a symbol of representation for minority groups, but representation without performance is meaningless. In our constitutional republic, we elect government officials to perform. In the realm of electoral politics, there are two types of voters. The rational and the irrational voter. Between the two, the irrational voter is the most prevalent. The irrational voter bases his vote on all aspects of a political candidate except the substance of the candidate's program. The rational voter, on the other hand, does not care about anything other than the candidate's program. In the United States, and we could even say in all the countries of the world, elections, whether presidential, legislative, or mayoral, are mostly determined by the irrational voter rather than the rational voter.

The irrational voter centered his decision to vote on two principles: pathos and ethos. Indeed, the irrational voter is not fundamentally concerned with the candidate's program. For this kind of voter, although the candidate's program may be important, it does not matter as much as the candidate's credibility and ability to emotionally connect with an audience. The irrational voter values more what the candidate could represent than his actual program. The irrational voter does not pay much attention to the candidate's program because the program may be too intellectually challenging to comprehend it fully since most voters are not intellectuals. Hence the irrational voter will not seek to look beyond the basic attributes that the candidates have to offer.

The rational voter, on the other hand, when voting for a candidate, prioritizes the logos and the ethos. This kind of voter is not concerned with the candidate's basic attributes. This type of voter focuses on the candidate's program and his credibility. Indeed, the candidate's program matters to the rational voter because the program is what determines which policies will be enforced if that candidate were elected. The rational voter wants to be sure that the policies proposed by the candidate are factual and evidence-based. For example, many people voted for Joe Biden because he asserted that he would implement a progressive income tax policy if elected. This policy sounds not only appealing but convincing as well because on theoretical grounds, it will tax the rich more and the poor would benefit more from it. But anyone who has done their research would know that the progressive income tax does not create long-term economic growth. Such a policy will force those who have the ability to create jobs, to leave the areas where jobs are needed the most. For the irrational voter though, a man like Joe Biden who proposes a progressive income tax is a symbolic representation of our democratic system because his tax plan portrays him as a man who supports working-class families. For the rational voter who thinks analytically about this issue, he would think that Biden's tax policy would hurt the economy because this policy will discourage any incentive to increase productivity and growth, which will eventually hurt the poor because the poor are those who need jobs the most. And there is a great deal of evidence that shows that a progressive income tax hurts the economy in the long-run.

The irrational voter would favor a candidate's external attributes rather than what he has to offer practically. Most members of the Black community vote that way. They base their vote on the candidate's social background rather than the substance of his program. This sort of thinking is why the Black community has always been disappointed with their leaders and the leaders of the Democratic Party.

Members of the Black community argue that the Democratic Party manipulates them, only uses them during every cycle to secure the Black vote. And yet, Black people keep voting for the Democratic Party every election cycle. This is what we call insanity. Democratic leaders are aware that so long as a Black person runs for political office, Black people will keep voting for the Democratic Party because most Blacks favor superficial representation over the substance of the candidate's policies.

6. BLACK CULTURE AND THE STOCK MARKET

In any market economy, there are mainly three pathways to building wealth. The first pathway is to own a business, the second pathway is to invest and own real estates, and the third pathway is to invest in the stock market and own stocks.

There is also a fourth pathway, but this pathway is done through rent-seeking.[169] This pathway is the path of politics. The pathway of politics to build wealth is the least honest and the least thorough approach because politicians build their wealth through taxation by increasing the size of government. As a result, politicians increase their wealth without creating new wealth for the society as a whole. Many Blacks have used the path of politics to become rich while they did not create any new wealth for the members of their constituency. A politician like former Congressman and civil rights activist John Lewis (1940-2020) who served in the United States House of Representatives from 1987 until his death, is a prime example of rent-seeking. When he took office in 1987, his salary was about $77,400 per annum.[170] Upon his

---

[169] Rent-seeking is the effort to increase one's share of existing wealth without creating new wealth. Rent-seeking results in reduced economic efficiency through misallocation of resources, reduced wealth-creation, lost government revenue, heightened income inequality, and potential national decline.
[170] United States Congress

137

death, he was earning $174,000 per annum. And his personal net worth is estimated at $300,000. Interestingly, John Lewis was never a business owner. He built his entire fortune in politics, meaning through the taxpayer's money.

John Lewis's Salary, 1987-2020

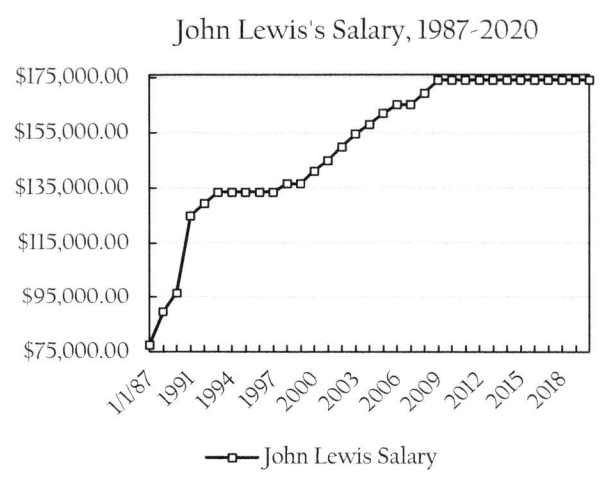

Figure 6.0. Source: United States Congress

Of the three aforementioned paths to creating wealth, the Black community has been mostly involved in the first two rather than the third one. Indeed, it is fair to asseverate that the Black community is very participative in the creation of businesses as well as in the investment and ownership of real estate. However, its participation in the stock market remains a very marginal involvement in that venue. Intriguingly enough, it is much easier to invest in the stock market than to start a business or invest in real estate.

1. Blacks in Business and Real Estate Ownership

   a) Blacks & Business Ownership

   According to the latest U.S. Census Bureau released in October 2021, Black Americans own approximately 134,567 businesses across the United States, with $133.7 billion in annual receipts, 1.3 million employees, and about $40.5 billion in annual payroll.[171] About 29.5 percent (39,705) of these businesses are in the healthcare and social assistance sector, which is the highest percentage of any minority group.[172] These results are certainly promising as more and more Blacks are creating small businesses all across the country although many factors remain relevant as to why not many Blacks are business owners.

   Owning a business is undeniably the surest path to creating wealth and secure financial freedom. But the creation of a business requires substantial capital and a whole lot of administrative procedures in order to finalize the operations. Depending on the type of business being created, the number of administrative hurdles augments. Over the past decade (2010-2020) nearly 38 percent of Black businesses have been in healthcare, social assistance, repair and maintenance, and personal and laundry services.[173] These industries alone require important capital in order to get started. For example, the

---

[171] "Census Bureau Release New Data on Minority-Owned, Veteran-Owned, and Women-Owned Business" *U.S. Census Bureau.* (2021).
[172] Ibid.
[173] "Interesting Facts & Statistics about Black-Owned Businesses." *The African American Business Guide.*

healthcare industry is an industry that needs substantial medical supplies in order for the business to operate on a daily basis. The administrative costs as well as the regulations enforced in such an industry make it difficult to operate plainly and sustainably. Despite the strong involvement of Blacks in the creation of businesses, the statistics show that Black business ownership has been relatively stagnant over the past decade.

Business Ownership by Race, 2010-2019

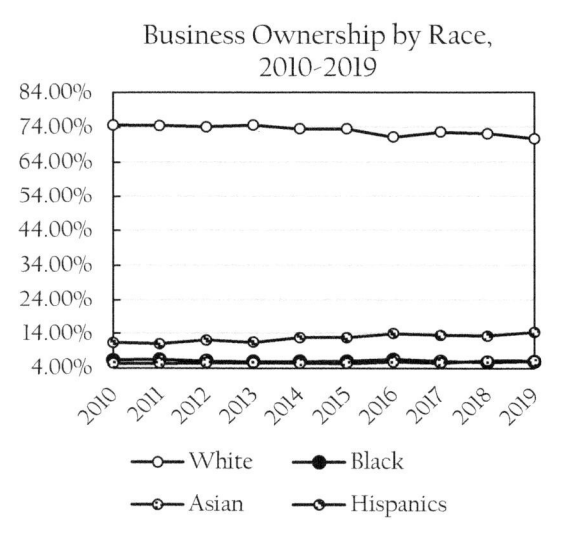

─○─ White ─●─ Black
─○─ Asian ─○─ Hispanics

Figure 6.1. Source: U.S. Census Bureau

Black-owned businesses tend to earn lower revenues in most industries and are overrepresented in low-growth, low-revenue industries such as food service and accommodations.[174] This gap in business activity contributes to an overall lower level of prosperity for Black families: the median White family's wealth is more than ten times the wealth of the median Black families.[175] The lower levels of business wealth among people of color, especially Blacks, have historically resulted from two factors: lower rates of business ownership and the fact that businesses owned by Blacks are smaller, on average than those owned by Whites.[176] The smaller size of Black-owned businesses is based on the historical limitations of industry sectors and the type of markets in which they operated.[177]

---

[174] Baboolall, David; Cook, Kelemwork; Noel, Nick; Stewart, Shelley; Yancy, Nina. "Building Supportive Ecosystems for Black-Owned US Businesses." *McKinsey & Company.* (2020)
[175] Ibid.
[176] "The Racial Gap in Business Ownership Explained in Four Charts." *Aspen Institute.* (2017)
[177] Aspen Institute, 2017

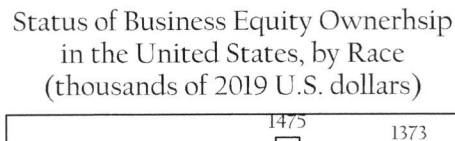

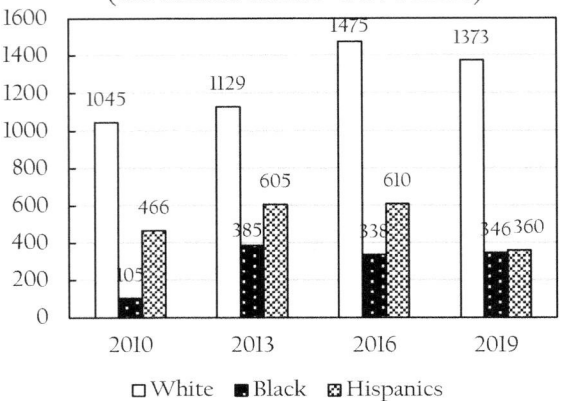

Status of Business Equity Ownerhsip in the United States, by Race (thousands of 2019 U.S. dollars)

Year	White	Black	Hispanics
2010	1045	105	466
2013	1129	385	605
2016	1475	338	610
2019	1373	346	360

Figure 6.2. Source: U.S. Census Bureau, Survey of Business Owners

b) *Blacks & Real Estate Ownership*

Real estate ownership, in the history of humanity, has always been perceived as the true symbol of wealth. It is even the culmination of the American dream, which is to own a piece of real estate.

When Thomas Jefferson affirmed in the Declaration of Independence that the fundamental and alienable rights of the individual are based on the right to life, the right to liberty, and the pursuit of happiness; especially the pursuit of happiness, he meant the right to property. The right to property is the cornerstone of the creation of wealth in America. However, in the early years of the republic, this fundamental right was restricted to the very few. As the United States evolved and became more of a democratic society than an aristocratic society, access to property was widened and more accessible to the general population.

The Black community has been very participative in the investment and acquisition of real estate as a means of creating generational wealth. When we observe the rate of homeownership by race since the 1990s, the White community has undeniably the highest rate of ownership among all races with no less than 70 percent.[178] The Black community, on the other hand, has been struggling to reach 50 percent of homeownership overall.

Homeownership by Race, 1994-2020

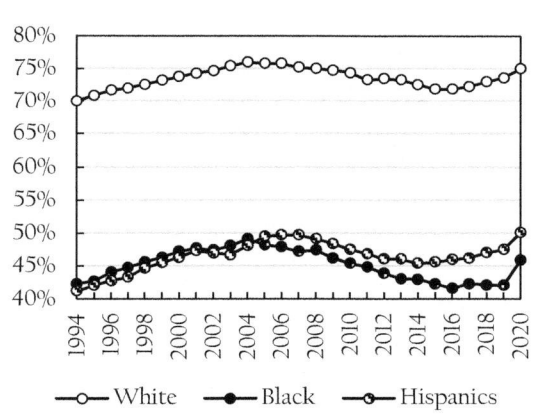

—o— White   —●— Black   —o— Hispanics

Figure 6.3. Source: U.S. Census Bureau

The U.S. homeownership rate is defined as the number of owner-occupied housing units divided by the total

---

[178] U.S. Census Bureau, (2020)

number of occupied housing units.[179] According to the data from the U.S. Census Bureau, the homeownership rate in the United States was 64 percent in 2019 and varies significantly by race and ethnicity.[180] In 2020, homeownership rate among White Americans was 75 percent, compared to 45 percent among Black Americans.[181] This 30 percentage point difference has been one of the largest gaps since the Census's time-series began in 1994.[182]

Homeownership is low within the Black community because the federal government, through its many agencies and threats of anti-discrimination lawsuits, forced banks and lenders to lower their standards for mortgage loans.[183] Lowering lending standards suggests higher risks of default.[184] As standards are lowered, more people from low-income communities take more loans out that they have trouble paying down the road due to a failure to make their mortgage payment on time.

Many social justice activists have argued that government intervention was necessary for the housing market to make housing more affordable for low-income communities such as the Black community. And the way to make housing more affordable to low-income communities is through rent control. The fallacy of this

---

[179] "Homeownership Rates Show That Black Americans are Currently The Least Likely Group to Own Homes." *USAFacts.* (2020)
[180] Ibid.
[181] Ibid.
[182] Ibid.
[183] Sowell, Thomas. "Bouncing Ball Politics." *Townhall.* (2013).
[184] Sowell, 2013

assertion is that rent control increases housing costs. The higher cost of housing leads to the restrictions of the number of houses that ought to be built. "Smart growth" laws restrict the expansion of home-building in suburban areas, and "open space" laws forbid the building of anything on land set aside in various areas.[185]

Rent control is meant to create or preserve housing units below-market rents without direct government subsidies to tenants.[186] It is presented as a solution to greedy landlords taking advantage of pinched renters in static housing markets.[187] Rent control increases the cost of housing because demand for housing simply exceeds supply. Rent control reduces the availability of housing which mainly hurts low-income communities. Whatever benefits do exist from rent control are poorly targeted, often missing people in need.[188] In New York, for example, the wealth transfer from rent-controlled landlords to tenants was disproportionately claimed by White, who are economically advantaged renters.[189] White renters in 2017 claimed a 36 percent discount on market-rate rents in New York City because of rent control, compared with 17 percent for Hispanic renters and 16 percent for Black renters.[190]

---

[185] Sowell, Thomas. "Urban Facts and Fallacies." *Economic Facts & Fallacies*. (2008). p. 25. Basic Books, New York. ISBN: 978-0-465-02203-8
[186] Hendrix, Michael. "Rent Control Does Not Make Housing More Affordable." *Issue Brief*. Manhattan Institute. (2020).
[187] Hendrix, 2020
[188] Hendrix, 2020
[189] Hendrix, 2020
[190] Hendrix, 2020

Lastly, rent control plays a major role in reducing a neighborhood's tax revenue. Schools in low-income neighborhoods are poorly managed and the quality of education is poor because these neighborhoods have very low tax revenues. Hence, these tax revenues cannot be transferred to the schools in order to improve their system. Rent control limits investment return and building quality, the assessed value of rent-controlled properties tends to decline, which lowers property-tax revenue.[191]

2. Blacks and the Lack of Investment in the Stock Market

The stock market is the least used platform by the Black community to build wealth, yet this platform is the easiest and the most lucrative platform to increase one's wealth sustainably.

According to the Federal Reserve data, only 34 percent of Black American households owned equity investments, as compared with 61 percent of White families.[192] The average value of stocks Black Americans owned amounted only to $14,400, nearly a quarter of what their White peers held.

---

[191] Hendrix, 2020

[192] Li, Yun. "Black Americans' Lack of Participation in the Stock Market Likely to Widen Post-Pandemic Wealth Gap." *CNBC*. (2022).

Share with Asset by Race

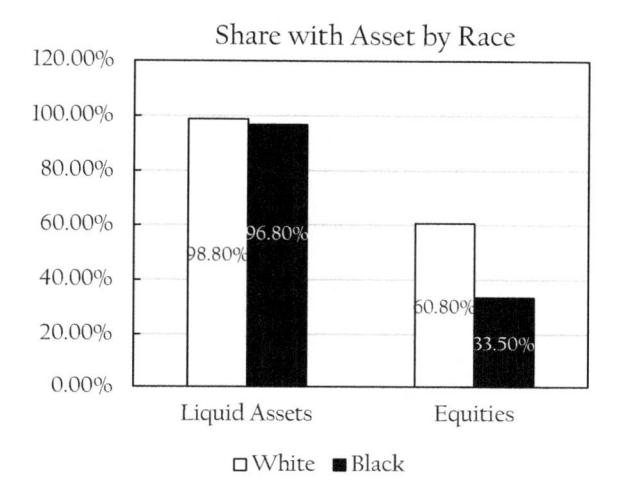

	Liquid Assets	Equities
White	98.80%	60.80%
Black	96.80%	33.50%

Figure 6.4. Source: Federal Reserve Board, 2019 Survey of Consumer Finances

Average Value of Stockownership by Race

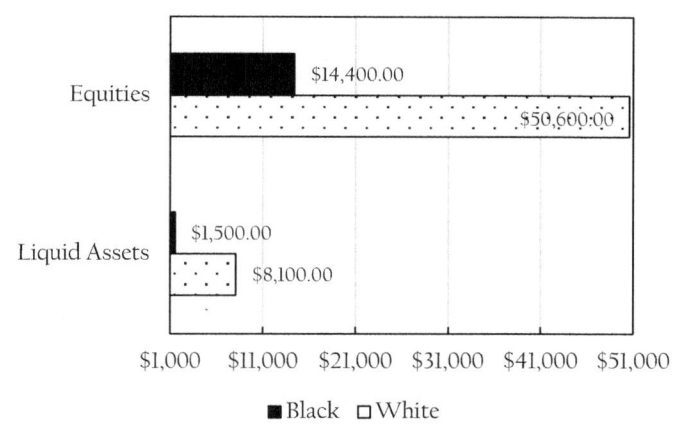

	Black	White
Equities	$14,400.00	$50,600.00
Liquid Assets	$1,500.00	$8,100.00

Figure 6.5. Source: Federal Reserve Board, 2019 Survey of Consumer Finances

Because Black households are less likely to be investing in the stock market and on every level less likely to be engaged in the financial system, they not only entered the pandemic with large gaps, but the likelihood is also that these gaps are going to widen coming out of the pandemic.[193] The primary way that Americans build wealth and invest is through retirement plans.[194] Many Black Americans missed out on the gains of the stock market because they often hold occupations where employers are unlikely to offer an employer-sponsored retirement plan.[195] Only 44 percent of Black Americans have retirement savings accounts with typically a balance of around $20,000, compared to 65 percent of White Americans, who have an average balance of 50,000, according to the Federal Reserve.[196]

The typical Black family has less than $13 in wealth for every $100 held by the typical White family.[197] The difference in stock ownership between Black and White households go back decades and they narrowed slightly between 2016 and 2019, according to the most recent data available from the Federal Reserve.[198] Rather than stocks, wealthier Black households are more likely to own assets that have a reputation for being safer, such as bonds, life insurance, or real estate.[199] This is because Black

---

[193] Li, 2022
[194] Li, 2022
[195] Li, 2022
[196] Li, 2022
[197] Choe, Stan. "Stocks are Soaring, and Most Black People are Missing Out." *ABC News.* (2020)
[198] Choe, 2020
[199] Choe, 2020

Americans tend to not trust assets that are not tangible.[200]

a) Cultural Bias Against the Stock Market

Unlike the stock market, businesses and real estate are tangible assets. And Blacks feel more comfortable investing in these kinds of assets because they have a greater likelihood to directly control the outcome while the stock market is not very much controllable.

The fundamental reason why Blacks find it difficult to invest in the stock market is that Blacks have a very high propensity to spend. Spending is a normal and natural thing to do. Everyone spends. But the main question is "spend on what kind of things?" Blacks have a high inclination to particularly spend in depreciative assets. Depreciative assets are types of assets whose cost exceeds their value. Depreciative assets are defined by their short-term span. Depreciative assets include vehicles, computers, manufacturing machinery, and luxury goods such as high-branded shoes, watches, clothes, glasses, and so on. These assets [depreciative assets] are costly, yet their value is short-lived.

Fashionable clothes, jewelry, flashy cars...They are all items of conspicuous consumption that give their owners status on the street.[201] Some groups, such as Blacks and Hispanics, seem to spend more on such emblems of

---

[200] Choe, 2020
[201] "Conspicuous Consumption and Race: Who Spends More on What." *Knowledge@Wharton*. University of Pennsylvania.

success than others.[202] Comedian Bill Cosby has long condemned his own Black community for spending too much on flashy goods at the expense of children's education.[203] Professor Nikolai Roussanov once asserted the following: "Blacks do spend more on these things—jewelry, clothing, and cars—that have something to with visibility. Is it just taste? Or does it have to do with a social status component?"[204] Many economists believe that valuable possessions visible to all are a signal of one's wealth, success, and status.[205] And this belief is correlated with hood culture, which has become the predominant culture in the Black community.

As was argued in chapter 4, hood culture is economically and socially corrosive because it relies on the use of depreciating assets to enhance wealth and social status. Investing in depreciating assets is costly for the investor because the limited lifespan of the value of that asset is compensated by its cost. Depreciative assets provide short-term satisfaction to the consumer that makes him feel fulfilled. However, the process to acquire this depreciative asset leaves the consumer in massive debt. For example, many members of the Black community enjoy driving flashy cars. But flashy cars such as a Rolls Royce are extremely expensive. A Rolls Royce costs on average $300,000. This is the cost of a house. Although possessing a Rolls Royce symbolizes having wealth, the value of a Rolls Royce is less significant than

---

[202] Ibid.
[203] Ibid.
[204] Ibid.
[205] Ibid.

that of a house because its value depreciates once it is used. The worst part is that once the debt of the car is paid off (let us say after five to six years or so) the car is longer valuable. Hence, the car would have already lost its value by the time the full payment of the debt is completed.

Stocks are not tangible assets and take time before their value appreciates. This is the process of any appreciative assets. The value of appreciative assets takes time to grow and reach maturity. This is not compatible with hood culture because hood culture is about spontaneity. However, it is much easier to invest in stocks than to invest in any other type of asset. Today, in the digital era, many brokerage firms do no longer require a minimum amount to depose in order to open a brokerage account. A person could invest as little as $10 in the stock market and expect decent returns after a substantial period of time. The hardest part about investing in stocks is to select the right stock. Selecting the right stock requires one to do his due diligence, which means analyzing the financial statements of a company one may be interested in before investing in it.

b) *Lack of Financial Literacy*

The unwillingness of Blacks to invest in the stock market may be due to a lack of financial literacy. As a matter of fact, according to the TIAA Institute-GFLEC Personal Finance Index (P-Fin Index), a survey that measures financial literacy, Blacks have demonstrated a low level.[206] The P-Fin Index showed that Black Americans only answered 38 percent of personal finance questions correctly compared to White Americans who answered 55 percent correctly.[207]

Black people received the highest scores in knowledge on borrowing and managing debt while their lowest score was in comprehending risk and uncertainty, insuring, investing, and go-to information sources.[208] The gap in financial knowledge between Black and White Americans may be partially due to educational opportunities.[209] Black Americans who are college-educated answered 53 percent of the P-Fin Index question correctly on average, compared with 24 percent among those with a high school or lower education level.[210]

---

[206] Perkins, Erin C. *Tackling Disparities in Finance for Black and African Americans.* MonkeyGeek. (2022).

[207] Yakoboski, Paul J. "Financial literacy, Wellness and Resilience Among African Americans." *TIAA Institute-GFLEC Personal Finance Index.* (2020). pp. 1-23

[208] Perkins, 2022

[209] Perkins, 2022

[210] *TIAA Institute-GFLEC Personal Finance Index,* 2020

Functional Financial Knowledge for Black Americans

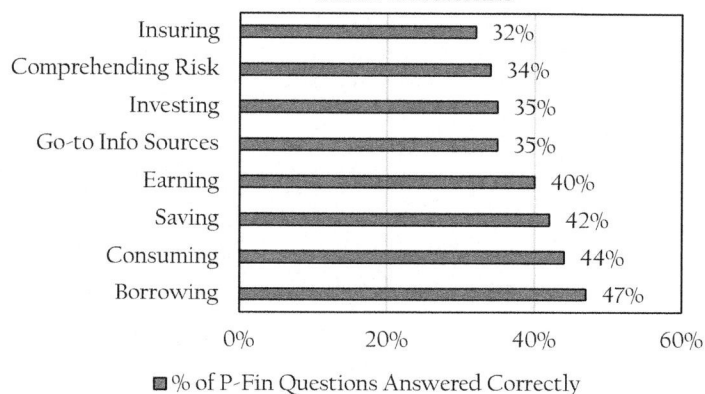

Category	%
Insuring	32%
Comprehending Risk	34%
Investing	35%
Go-to Info Sources	35%
Earning	40%
Saving	42%
Consuming	44%
Borrowing	47%

■ % of P-Fin Questions Answered Correctly

Figure 6.6. Source: TIAA Institute GFLEC Personal Finance Index

This analysis could lead us to theorize that there could be a relationship between educational attainment and stock ownership. Since those who have a college degree have a better understanding of financial processes and structures, we could then hypothesize that educated Blacks are more likely to invest more extensively in the stock market than those who have a lower level of education. In testing this relationship statistically, we see that our hypothesis is consistent with the data.[211] We can

---

[211] We statistically test the relationship between educational attainment for Blacks who have completed a college degree, and Black households that own stocks. We initially intended to use the simple linear regression (SLR) to test this hypothesis. However, the lack of linearity prevented us from using the SLR. Hence, a linear regression would not fit in the data. Since the relationship between dependent variable and predictor is not linear, we then used polynomial regression in order to capture all observations that are on

see from figure 6.7. that there is a strong positive correlation between educational attainment and stock ownership for Blacks ($R^2 = 0.8253$). We are surely aware that correlation is not causation. We are, in no way, implying that educational attainment is the cause that led to Black households owning stocks. However, this correlation shows that educational attainment is a preponderant factor in the decision-making process of Black households to own stocks.

It is interesting to see that one of the main reasons why many White American households are so financially prosperous is because they heavily invest in stocks. In point of fact, many of the so-called alternative investment vehicles such as hedge funds, mutual funds, or investment funds, are run by White Americans. For example, Jim Simons, Ken Griffin, Ray Dalio, George Soros, Carl Icahn, Steve Cohen, David Tepper, Israel Englander, Cliff

---

the scatterplot. The statistical model can be denoted as $Y = \beta_0 + \beta_1 X_1 + \beta_2 X_1^2 + \beta_3 X_1^3 + \varepsilon$ where (Y), which is our dependent variable, represents the percentage of Black household owning stocks, and (X_1), which is our predictor, represents the percentage of Black Americans who completed a college degree. (X_1^2) and (X_1^3) are the new predictors added to the initial predictor. These predictors are simply the original predictor that has been extrapolated because the relationship between the dependent variable and the predictor is curvilinear. Lastly, (ε) represents the error term. The data used to test our hypotheses were mainly obtained from the Pew Research Center and the Federal Reserve Board. We built a cross-sectional dataset of 51 observations (n=51). After applying descriptive and inferential statistical methods, we found that the relationship between the two variables was statistically significant with a p-value significantly below 5% (p-value = 0.004). This, henceforth, shows that there is sufficient evidence against the null hypothesis.

Asness...etc., just to name a few, are all White Americans who are hedge fund managers and billionaires. They comprehended that they could use the stock market to create a lot of wealth for their clients and for themselves. Today, these people aforementioned, control a substantial portion of the wealth created in the United States. Their ability to generate so much wealth is due to the fact that they increase their financial literacy. Jim Simons, for example, who is the richest hedge fund manager in the world ($24.4 billion according to Forbes) is not a trained financial professional. He is a trained mathematician who used his mathematical knowledge and skills to understand how the stock market works and took advantage of market patterns to make a lot of money. He applied mathematical and statistical techniques to anticipate hidden market movements, which enabled him to beat the market consistently.

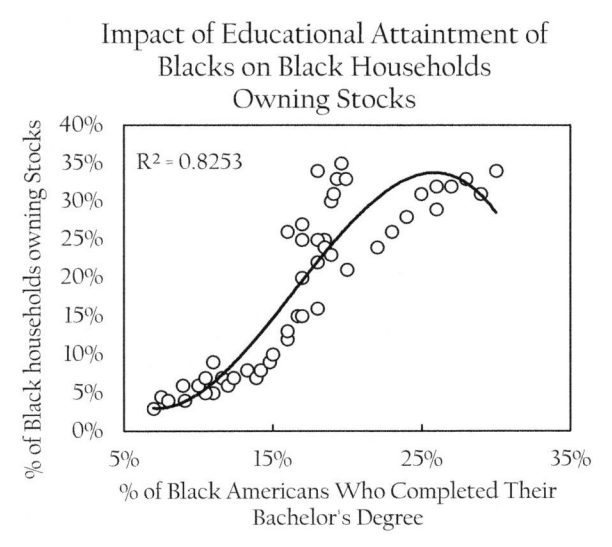

Impact of Educational Attaintment of Blacks on Black Households Owning Stocks

$R^2 = 0.8253$

% of Black Americans Who Completed Their Bachelor's Degree

Figure 6.7. Source: Author's regression analysis

There are not enough Blacks involved in the American financial system. And this is one of the reasons why the racial gap continues to widen between Whites and Blacks. White Americans are involved and have a deep understanding of the stock market and the financial system while Blacks are lacking these two crucial elements. It is undeniable that Blacks will do enormously better if they invest more in the stock market.

The wealthiest households in America mainly built their fortune from their investments in various financial securities through the stock market. They used the stock market to create generational wealth. The first rule of building wealth is to save, then invest. It will be very hard for the Black community to invest more rigorously in the stock market with such current spending habits that most members of the community display.

Investing requires a lot of financial discipline such as having a clear and concise budget, drastically cutting spending, living below one's financial means...etc. In short, investing requires one to be frugal whereas hood culture is anti-frugal. And this is a problem that the Black community will have to address if it wants to avoid generational poverty. Without thorough financial literacy and strong saving habits, generational poverty will likely remain a cultural feature of the Black community. The stock market is a very good resource to build wealth, and the Black community could build substantial wealth on this platform if it changes its spending habits.

7. BLACK CULTURE & INFRASTURCTURES

It is undeniable that for a community to develop economically and socially, it must have an economic system on which its members can rely. This means that this community must have the necessary infrastructures so that its economy would operate efficiently. The Black community is the least advanced socioeconomically advanced community because it does not have an economic system on which its members could rely since it lacks infrastructures.

An economy needs reliable infrastructures to connect the supply chain and efficiently move goods and services across borders.[212] Infrastructures connect households across metropolitan areas to higher qualities opportunities for employment, healthcare, and education.[213] The most productive and advanced communities do have the infrastructures required to make the economy of their community work. What are these infrastructures? Banks, schools, hospitals, law firms, pharmacies, transportation companies, telecommunication companies, libraries, factories, and so

---

[212] Puentes, Robert. "Why Infrastructure Matters: Rotten Roads, Bum Economy." *Brookings Institute*. (2015).
[213] Puentes, 2015

on. These infrastructures aforementioned are what make an economy work.

When we look at all the communities living in the United States, the most advanced ones have these listed infrastructures in place. More importantly, the advanced communities continuously invest in these infrastructures. Does the Black community have absolutely no infrastructure at all? It certainly does. The community has Black-owned banks, Black-owned hospitals, Black-owned schools...etc. The conundrum here is that Black infrastructures are not high-quality infrastructures. It does not mean that because a set of infrastructures are Black-owned, therefore they are of poor quality. This is not what this assertion implied. Black infrastructures do not lack for quality or service per se. What this contention means, on the other hand, is that Black-owned infrastructures are of poor quality because the community does not invest enough in them. There is a critical lack of investment in Black infrastructures. A resource that receives limited investment ends up becoming of poor quality because its lack of investment prevents the improvement of its quality.

1. **The Problem of Government's Subsidization of Black Infrastructures**

In President Biden's release statement regarding his infrastructure bill, he asseverated that his bill would use the government's purchasing power to drive an additional $100 billion to small disadvantaged business owners. The White House described its intent to subsidize Black businesses as the following:

"The federal government is the largest consumer of goods in the world, buying everything from software to elevator services to financial and asset management, Federal procurement is one of our most powerful tools to advance equity and build wealth in underserved communities. And yet, just roughly 10 percent of federal agencies' total eligible contracting dollars typically go to small disadvantaged businesses (SDB), a category under federal law for which Black-owned, Latino-owned, and other minority-owned businesses are presumed to qualify. Increasing federal spending with these businesses will help more Americans realize their entrepreneurial dreams and help narrow racial wealth gaps. In 2019, for instance, the gap in business ownership between Blacks and Latino households, relative to White households, accounted for 25 percent of the overall racial wealth gap between these groups."[214]

Reading this statement, one can only be flattered by the ambitions set out by President Biden to help the Black community invest in its infrastructures in order to build its collective wealth. On the surface, it is undeniable that these intentions are of goodwill. However, we shall never judge a policy by its intentions but by the results it generates. The trap is that many members of the Black community judged Biden's policy by its intention rather than its results.

Biden's policy has not yet been fully implemented for us to judge its effects thoroughly on its sole merits. But compelling historical evidence suffice to give us at least an idea of the potential outcome of that policy. It is more

---

[214] President Biden. "Fact Sheet: Biden-Harris Administration Announces New Actions to Build Black Wealth and Narrow the Racial Wealth Gap." *Statements and Releases.* (2021). The White House.

or less easy to predict that this policy will not produce the expected fallouts for the simple reason that government subsidization of businesses will prevent Black-owned businesses and infrastructures from thriving and creating the wealth that is supposed to establish the economic powerbase of the Black community.

The problem with state subsidization is that when government subsidizes businesses, it weakens profit- and-loss signals in the economy and undermines market- based entrepreneurship.[215] Government subsidization is generally pernicious for three reasons: (1) government lacks the incentives to manage funds that private investors have; (2) giving subsidies to some businesses puts other businesses that do not receive such subsidies at a disadvantage, distorting investment and other economic activity; and (3) the existence of government subsidies increases the incentive to lobby and the power of special interest groups.[216]

Even with the best of intentions, elected officials and bureaucrats simply do not possess the proper incentives to manage taxpayers' money prudently.[217] They are not rewarded when they maximize consumer value; nor are they punished when they take unnecessary risks or fail to minimize costs.[218] Government actors operate with

---

[215] De Rugy, Veronique. *Subsidies Are the Problem, Not the Solution, for Innovation in Energy.* (2015). Mercatus Center—George Mason University. pp. 1-5
[216] Ibid. p. 2
[217] Ibid. p. 2
[218] Ibid. p. 2

limited knowledge.[219] While individuals acting in markets are able to use price signals to guide decisions.[220] When a privately-owned company fails, the owner and investors of the company are directly affected by the cost of that failure that they must bear. When a government program fails, bureaucrats pay no price for making the wrong decisions that led to the program's failure. The only loser in the failure of a government program is the taxpayer because the government will require taxes to be raised in order to create a new program that will replace the failed one.

By aiding particular businesses and industries, subsidies put other businesses and industries at a disadvantage.[221] This market distortion generates losses to the economy that are not easily seen and thus generally are not considered by policymakers.[222] When government starts choosing industries and technologies to subsidize, it often makes bad decisions at taxpayer expense, because policymakers possess no special knowledge that allows them to allocate capital more efficiently than markets.[223] Government subsidies create a healthy—and sometimes corrupt—relationship between commercial interests and the government.[224] The more government has intervened in a given market, the more lobbying activity has been generated—the more subsidies that it hands out to businesses, the more

---

[219] Ibid. p. 2
[220] Ibid. p. 2
[221] Ibid. p. 3
[222] Ibid. p. 3
[223] Ibid. p. 3
[224] Ibid. p. 4

pressure policymakers face to keep the federal spigot flowing.[225] As the number of lobbyists grows, more economic decisions are made on the basis of politics, and more resources are misallocated.[226]

The infrastructure policy of President Biden will not make a difference in improving Black infrastructures since government lacks the profit motive required to allocate capital efficiently. Moreover, Black infrastructures so far are the least profitable, therefore there is a strong likelihood that the federal government may not do what is necessary to improve the quality of these infrastructures. One clear yet decisive example of how government subsidization failed the Black community is in the housing market.

Histories of Black urban life have focused on public housing, housing discrimination, redlining, and the rise and fall of tenants' rights movements.[227] In her book *Race for Profit*, Pulitzer Prize-winning author Keenaga-Yamahtta Taylor explained how the federal government and bankers manipulated tens of thousands of Black people through a program of predatory lending that claimed to empower Black homeowners but ultimately pushed them into greater financial insecurity.[228] Agencies like the Federal Housing Administration (FHA) and the

---

[225] Ibid. p. 4
[226] Ibid. p. 4
[227] Chatelain, Marcia. "The Burning House." *The Nation.* (2020).
[228] Taylor, Keeanga-Yamahtta. *Race for Profit: How Banks and the Real Estate Industry Undermined Black Homeownership (Justice, Power, and Politics).* University of North Carolina Press. (2019). ISBN: 978-1469653679

Department of Housing and Urban Development (HUD) may have been founded to "transform low-income renters into low-income homeowners," Taylor writes, but they ended up squeezing poor Black homeowners while creating lucrative financial instruments for lenders and real interests.[229] Housing and homeownership are crucial infrastructures in the Black community. This instance of government subsidization clearly epitomized how government policies designed to help Blacks always end up hurting them.

2. Improving Black Infrastructures

The quality of Black infrastructures can greatly improve and become more profitable if the right investments are made in the chief infrastructures that represent the engine of the community. It is, however, important to stress the two essential reasons why Black businesses lack funding to build and maintain infrastructures are based on low asset acquisition and low credit scores. The following data show the median value of assets held by different racial and ethnic groups, as well as the average credit score by different racial and ethnic groups. As we observe the data, we see that in both figures (figures 7.0. & 7.1.) Blacks have the lowest assets values especially, in homeownership, business ownership, while they slightly do better than Hispanics on financial instruments and have the same median value asset for their requirement accounts as them. On credit scores, Blacks have the lowest score among different ethnic groups.

---

[229] Chatelain, 2020

Median Value of Assets Held by Different Racial and Ethnic Groups

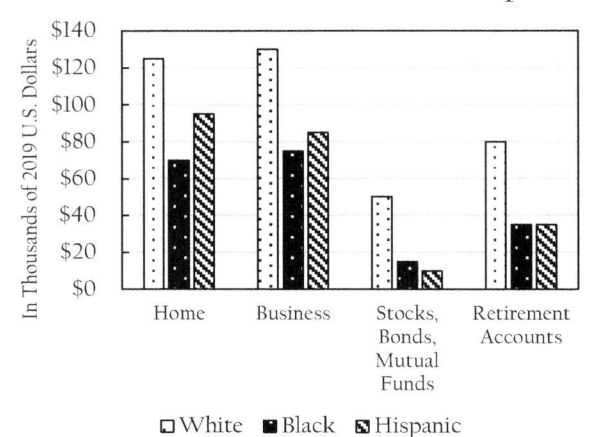

Figure 7.0. Source: Federal Reserve Data

Average Credit Score by Racial Groups

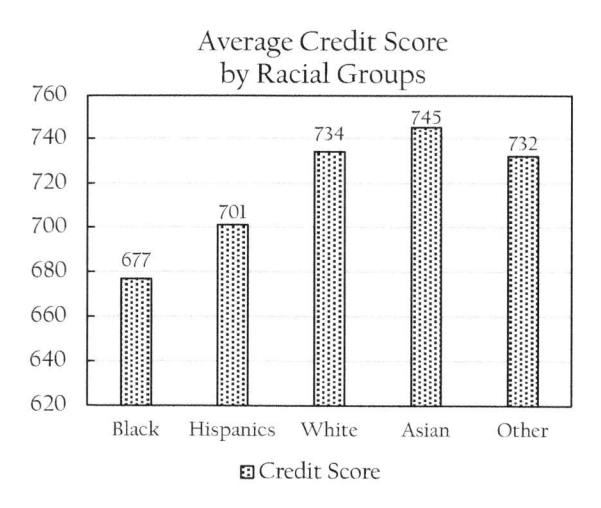

Group	Credit Score
Black	677
Hispanics	701
White	734
Asian	745
Other	732

Figure 7.1. Source: Shift Credit Card Processing & U.S. Federal Reserve Data

Are Black infrastructures underfunded because they are Black-owned? Certainly not. What matters to banks and lenders is the ability of the debtor to repay his debt. The ability to obtain a loan from a bank or an investor is determined by the assets that the debtor owns as well as his credit score. During the loan acquisition process, banks and lenders generally require the debtor to pledge a high-value asset that would serve as collateral damage. This collateral damage gives the creditor (banks and lenders) the legal right to seize the debtor's asset (the collateral damage) in case of failure to repay the debt. Low credit scores, as well as the low value of Black-owned assets, make banks and lenders reluctant to invest in Black-owned businesses.

Blacks have low-value assets because they have low incomes. These low incomes are mainly related to low-pay jobs available in low-income neighborhoods. Thus, the availability of low-paid jobs is based on the poor quality of education, which is mainly due to low local tax revenue as well as the low standard of living in Black neighborhoods. We can see that it is an entire cycle of poverty that prevents many Black-owned businesses to secure important funding. Furthermore, when banks and lenders decide to grant a loan to a Black-owned business, they do so with high-interest rates on the loan to maximize the profit that could be generated from the failure of the reimbursement.

It is preponderant to asseverate that 99 percent of Black-owned businesses are small businesses and 96 percent of these 99 percent are sole proprietorships (unincorporated businesses owned and operated by one individual) compared to 79.9 percent of non-Black-owned businesses.[230] Small businesses alone cannot develop the infrastructures that the economy of a community needs to properly function. So, the main question here is to know how the Black community could improve its infrastructures without having to be subsidized by the federal government?

The Black community has a good number of influential individuals who alone hold the financial resources that the community needs to improve its infrastructures. The majority of wealthy Black Americans are in the entertainment industry. Hip-hop artists such as Jay-Z, Puff Daddy, Snoop Dogg, Kanye West, Beyonce, or Nicky Minaj; movie actors and Television personalities such as Oprah Winfrey, Viola Davis, Denzel Washington, or Samuel L. Jackson; and athletes such as Lebron James, the Williams sisters, or Michael Jordan; are all multi-millionaires and billionaires. Each of these individuals mentioned can alone renovate an entire Black neighborhood. These are people we all look up to in the community as a model of success. Yet not many of them have done so to improve the infrastructures of the community. Jay-Z, for example, has a net worth of $1.4 billion according to Forbes. If he hypothetically allocates 25 percent of his wealth (which is $350 million) into the investment of infrastructures such as schools and hospitals in some Black neighborhoods in New York, such an investment will utterly help schoolteachers and

---

[230] Perry, Andre M.; Boyea-Robinson, Tynesia; Romer, Carl. "How Black-owned businesses can make the most out of the Biden infrastructure plan?" *Brookings Institute.* (2021).

medical professionals in these neighborhoods to work with good-quality supplies. This will overall improve the quality of the infrastructures and Jay-Z will still be a billionaire. Kanye West is another influential person who is worth $1.8 billion according to Forbes. If Kanye allocates the same percentage of his wealth as Jay-Z hypothetically did into the investment of infrastructures in the Black community, this will undeniably help the community to rely on itself rather than the government or another community. We believe that the infrastructures of the community can be improved through self-reliance, self-sufficiency, and a property-based approach. Those at the top of the community who have the financial means to invest in Black-owned infrastructures shall be incentivized to do.

The community should focus the investment of its infrastructures mainly on Black-owned banks. There are only forty-two Black-owned banks in the United States. To understand why Black-owned banks matter, it is critical to recognize the role banks play in the financial system of a community and a nation as a whole.[231] Banks are the institutions that manage money, its demand, and supply.[232] They usually provide financial services such as access to a checking account, allowing for the safe storage of an individual's funds, accepting monetary deposits, offering loans for both individuals and businesses looking

---

[231] Friedman, Milton. "The Role of Monetary Policy." *The American Economic Review.* Vol. 58, No. 1. (1968). pp. 1-17
[232] Ibid. p. 1

for crucial financial purchases...etc.[233] In addition to the conventional financial services they offer, banks offer programs of financial literacy for low-income communities.[234] Black-owned businesses offer an alternative for residents who have been consistently discriminated against by other financial institutions.[235] They have typically provided more money to borrowers living in low- and moderate-income census tracts in the last decade than other banks and Black-owned banks are also willing to tolerate higher levels of risk than alternative institutions.[236] The specificity of Black-owned banks is that they mainly lend to small Black-owned businesses. As we know, small Black-owned businesses do not have substantial leverage to expand the scope of the infrastructures of the community.

What ought to be done then is to invest more in Black-owned banks so that these banks can lend colossal capital to small Black-owned businesses which will allow them to scale faster and become multinational companies. In order for small Black-owned businesses to qualify for bank business loans, they must convert from sole proprietorship to a corporation or limited liability company (LLC) structure. Multinational companies are the ones that develop the infrastructures of the community and society at large. Small businesses in

---

[233] Dugyala, Rishika "US Banks teach financial literacy with Hands-on Experience." *Reuters.* (2018)
[234] Dugyala, 2018
[235] Neal, Michael; Walsh, John. *The Potential and Limits of Black-Owned Banks.* Urban Institute. (2020), pp. 1-16
[236] Ibid. p. 2

general have a greater propensity to fail than corporations and multinationals would. This is because corporations have sufficient capital to hire great labor, technologies, and resources to continue the scaling process while a small business does not have access to such vast amounts of capital. Our proposition to invest in Black-owned banks can be illustrated by the following model:

**Community-based
Infrastructural Development Model**

```
Wealthy Black Individuals → Black-Owned Banks → Small Black-owned businesses → Small Black-owned Business Scaled to Corporation → Creation of New Black Infrastructures
```

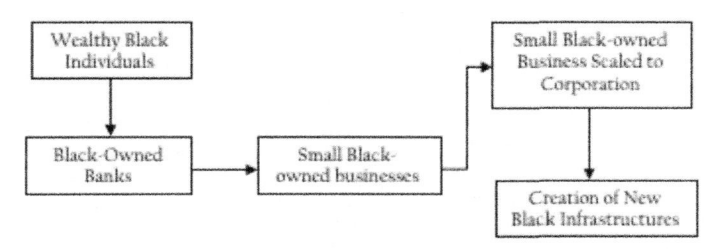

Figure 7.2

8. BLACK CULTURE, CRIME & GENERATIONAL POVERTY

In chapter 4, we elaborated on some of the counterproductive habits of hood culture in the Black community such as hip-hop culture, sexual promiscuity, and aversion to work. However, we had not addressed perhaps the most decisive of these counterproductive behaviors which is the problem of crime in the Black community. The most blatant stigma attributed to the Black community is the number of crimes that occur per day and capita in Black neighborhoods. It is important to reiterate once again that in American culture, being Black is associated with poverty and crime.

It is undeniable that the Black community has the highest crime rate among all the different racial and ethnic groups in the United States. According to the Federal Bureau of Investigation (FBI), Black Americans accounted for 55.9 percent of all homicide offenders in 2019, while Whites 41.1 percent.[237] Among homicide victims in 2019 where the race was known, 54.7 percent were Black, while 42.3 percent were White.[238] The FBI asserts that during that same year, the per-capita offending rate for Blacks was roughly eight times higher

---

[237] "2019 Crime in the United States," *Federal Bureau of Investigation.* (2019).
[238] Ibid.

than that of Whites, and their victim rate was similar.[239] As we can see in the data regarding the prevalence rate of violent crime in the United States from 2014 to 2019 by race, Blacks have been leading despite a slow decrease between 2015 and 2018. In 2019, Hispanics had a higher rate of prevalence of violent crime than Blacks. This difference, however, was not substantial.

Prevalence Rate of Violent Crime in the United States from 2014 to 2019, by Race/Ethnicty

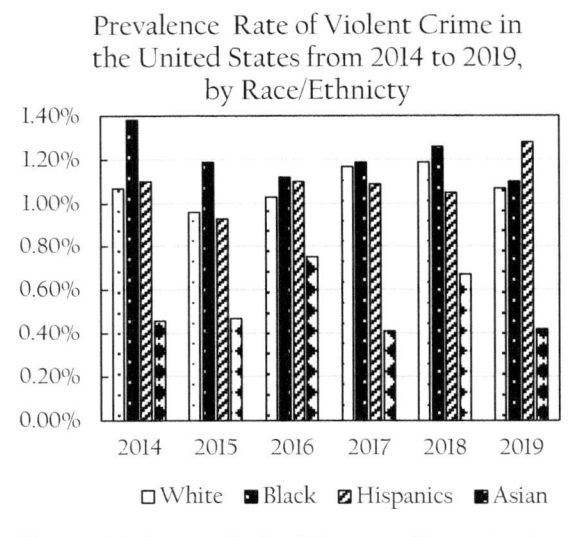

□ White ■ Black ▨ Hispanics ■ Asian

Figure 8.0. Source: Federal Bureau of Investigation

The purpose of this chapter is to understand where this strong inclination for crime in the Black community comes from. Our hypothesis suggests that those high crimes rates are linked to violence, disregard and disrespect for property rights, lawlessness, and neglect for education, all of which are counterproductive

---

[239] Ibid.

behaviors of hood culture which lead to prison and generational poverty.

1. Violence, Lawlessness, & Violation of Property Rights

Why is there so much crime and violence in most Black neighborhoods? We maintain that the cause of violence and rampant crime in Black neighborhoods is based on hood culture, which is a culture that has no regard and consideration for property rights, and the rule of law. In short, it is a culture of lawlessness that praises animalistic behaviors.

Centuries before "Black pride" became a fashionable phrase, there was cracker pride—and it was very much the same kind of pride.[240] It was not pride in any particular achievement or set of behavioral standards or moral principles adhered to.[241] It was instead a touchiness about anything that might be even remotely construed as a personal slight, much less an insult, combined with a willingness to erupt into violence over it.[242]

Violence is an intrinsic behavior of hood culture. It is a behavior that dominates Black neighborhoods because it is seen as the method of imposing authority in a culture of lawlessness. Violence in hood culture is very similar to the state of nature described by Thomas Hobbes in his groundbreaking book, *The Leviathan*, published in 1651. In

---

[240] Sowell, Thomas. "Black Redneck and White Liberals." *Black Rednecks and White Liberals.* (2005). p. 7. Basic Books, New York. ISBN: 978-1594031434
[241] Ibid. p. 7
[242] Ibid. p. 7

his work, Hobbes described the state of nature as a miserable state of war in which none of our important human ends are reliably realizable.[243] In his own words, he claimed that the state of nature was "a state of war of all against all, and which is worst of all, continual fear, and danger of violent death, and the life of man, solitary, poor nasty, brutish, and short."[244]

Thomas Hobbes explained that the state of nature is a state of perpetual war where individuals live in primitive instincts, that is to say, that the law of the strongest was the law that governed the state of nature. And the law of the strongest can only be imposed through violence. In the Hobbesian state of nature, an individual can deprive another individual of his property and there was no mediator or higher authority to repair the injustice done since it was the doctrine of the law of the strongest which dominated the state of nature.

In primitive groups, violence was the basis of hierarchical structure in these groups. The one to impose violence in the community is the one to impose his rules that others must abide by if they want to survive. Hood culture operates exactly this way. The most violent gets to impose his rules on the weaker members of the community.

---

[243] Dyson. R.W. "Nature, Morality and Realism: The Political Philosophy of Thomas Hobbes" *Natural Law and Political Realism in the History of Political Thought: Volume II—From the Seventeenth to the Twenty-First Century.* (2007). p. 1-35. Peter Lang Publishing, New York. ISBN: 978-0820488820
[244] Ibid. p. 15

This culture of lawlessness in Black neighborhoods is mirrored by gang activity. Gangs are the ones that rule low-income Black neighborhoods. Gangs practice excessive vandalism as well as shootings in the community. They impose terror among the community, and even those who want nothing to do with gang feuds are sadly forced to live in this torment as they live in these neighborhoods. Shootings and destruction of property occur systematically in low-income Black neighborhoods. For example, the city of Chicago has gained a notorious reputation for being the most infamous city for gang violence. The following data show that between 2019 and 2020, most of the violent crimes were related to shooting victims. Indeed, Chicago has seen a 43 percent increase in killings between 2019 and 2020, which is an alarming augmentation that incentivizes the adherence of more Blacks in gangs.

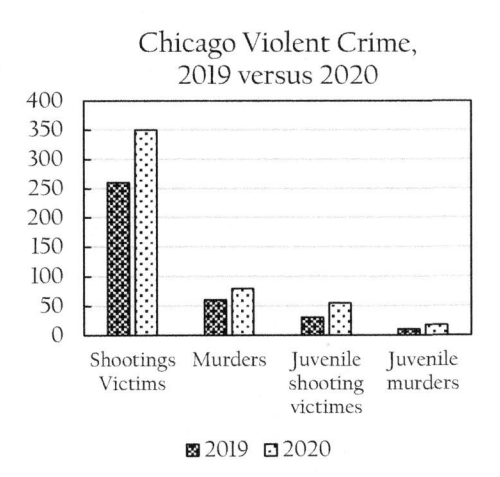

Figure 8.1. Source: Chicago Police Department

Most of the gang members are relatively young. The data illustrate that nearly 33,000 Chicago gang members are juveniles since 1999 with 24.6 percent who are 17 years old or younger, and 34.3 percent are between 18 and 24 years old.[245]

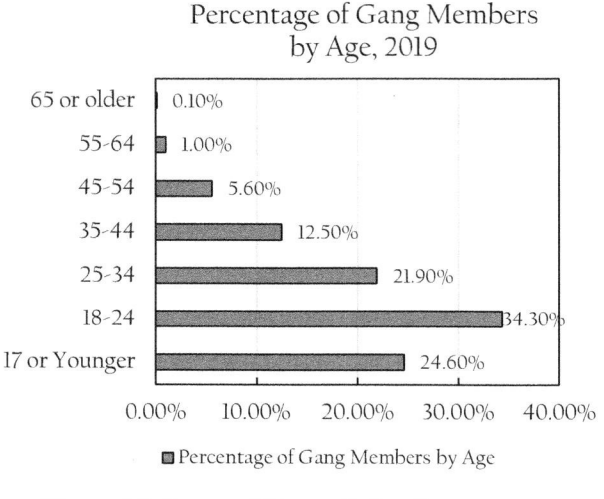

Percentage of Gang Members by Age, 2019

Age	Percentage
65 or older	0.10%
55-64	1.00%
45-54	5.60%
35-44	12.50%
25-34	21.90%
18-24	34.30%
17 or Younger	24.60%

Figure 8.2. Source: Chicago Police Department

Most of these young people who join gangs usually do not do so of their own accord. They do it under the influence of their environment. In low-income Black neighborhoods, joining a gang is the way to obtain power and respect. In his presentation at a conference, Rob Aspholm argued that Black American gangs today are

---

[245] Sweeny, Annie; Fry, Paige. "Nearly 33,000 juveniles arrested over last two decades labeled as gang members by Chicago Police." *Chicago Tribune* (2018).

vastly different from their 20th-century counterparts.[246] Professor Aspholm found that many new horizontal gangs have strong neighborhood loyalty and are often named after a slain clique member, or "homeboy."[247] These new cliques have eschewed the traditional vertical command structures and formal rules.[248] Violence is typically initiated by individuals and not commanded by gang leaders as it was in the past.[249] The new gangs have developed new territorial enemies and the old rivalries have been rendered largely meaningless.[250] The following table shows the two gang paradigms of their street organizations and cliques.

Characteristic of Violence	Street Organization/Gang Nation	Neighborhood Gang/Clique
Scope of gang wars	Cross-neighborhood	Local
Basis for gang wars	Control of drug markets, power, gang ideologies	Interpersonal conflicts and vendettas
Basis for alliances	Gang affiliation	Personal relationships common enemies
Meaning of violence	Instrumental, ideological	Expressive-vengeance, identity, meaning-making

---

[246] Hagedorn, John; Aspholm, Roberto; Cordova, Teresa; Papachristos, Andrew; Williams, Lance. *Fracturing of Gangs and Violence: A Research-Based Reorientation of Violence Prevention and Intervention Policy*. Great Cities Institute University of Illinois at Chicago. (2019). pp. 1-28
[247] Ibid. p. 7
[248] Ibid. p. 8
[249] Ibid. p. 8
[250] Ibid. p. 8

Violence controlled by	Gang leadership	Individual gang members
Regulation/predictability of violence	Relatively high	Very low

Table 8.0. Source: Rob Aspholm, Great Cities Institute University of Illinois at Chicago

Compared with the previous century where gang activities were centered around the control of the drug market across neighborhoods, 21st-century gangs in Chicago focus on personal vendettas, and the crime taking place is within the neighborhood rather than a rivalry between different neighborhoods. This is even worse because it accentuates the irrationality of gang members' actions. As most gang members are very young, young criminals are compromising their socioeconomic fate to one day become self-sufficient and productive members of society. This jeopardy sets them to generational poverty.

2. Unemployment, Poverty, and Crime

It is undeniable that there is an intrinsic link between poverty and crime. The poorer people are, the more likely they turn to criminal activities as a means of survival and sustentation. This is perfectly logical. If crime and violence are unconditional aspects of generational poverty, it is important to ask what crime leads to poverty in the first place?

We argue that unemployment, especially youth unemployment, is primarily the driving factor for raising crime in urban areas, and especially in low-income Black neighborhoods within those urban areas. Since the city of Chicago remains the most nationally known place for its high level of crime, we decided to test our hypothesis statistically by focusing on the relationship between the rate of unemployment in every Chicago neighborhood as well and the crime rate in each of these neighborhoods.[251]

---

[251] We used the linear regression to test our hypothesis. The model could be denoted as: **Crime** = $\beta_0 + \beta_1 \text{YUEMP} + \varepsilon$ where Crime is our dependent variable, and (YUEMP), which is the predictor, represents youth employment rate. Youth unemployment takes into account people between 16 and 24 years old. Our data contains 77 observations (n=77). Each observation represents a neighborhood in the City of Chicago. The data were extracted from Chicago Data Portal and the Chicago Police Department. In assessing the descriptive statistics of the data, we saw that both variables (dependent and predictor) were extremely skewed. To avoid any potential misleading results, we applied the logarithm transformation to ensure that the values of both variables would fit in the data. The result of our regression suggests that the relationship between youth unemployment and crime in the city of Chicago is statistically very significant ($p < 0.001$) ($p = 1.0063 \times 10^{-9}$). Although there is a moderately strong correlation between the predictor and the dependent variable ($R = 0.627$), the proportion of the variance in the response variable that can be explained by the predictor is only of 39.39% ($R^2 = 0.3939$). In other words, 39.39% of the variation in crime rate can be explained by the rate of youth unemployment.

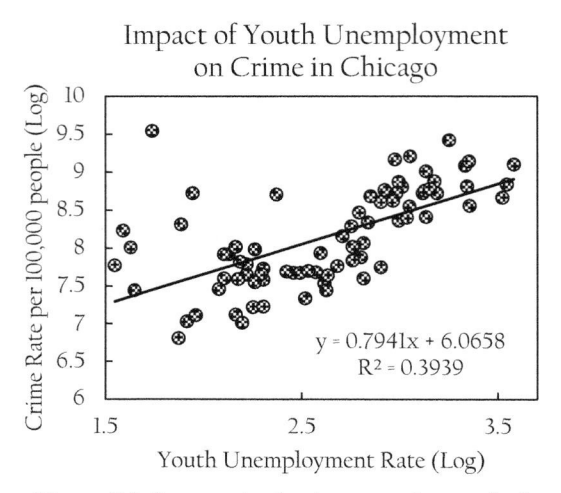

Impact of Youth Unemployment on Crime in Chicago

$y = 0.7941x + 6.0658$
$R^2 = 0.3939$

Figure 8.3. Source: Author's regression analysis

The results of our regression analysis suggest that there is strong evidence against the null hypothesis as the p-value shows the relationship between youth unemployment rate and crime rate is statistically very significant. However, only 39 percent of the variation in crime can be explained by the rate of youth unemployment. We can subsequently infer that youth unemployment, although undeniably important in understanding the accentuation of poverty in the city of Chicago, is not the fundamental factor that incentivizes crime in that city. This does not mean, however, that youth unemployment does not play a role in generational poverty in Chicago Black neighborhoods. On the contrary, data from the Federal Reserve of Chicago suggest that Blacks among unemployed youth account for more than 50 percent in Chicago while Hispanics account for 30 percent, Whites for less than 10 percent, and Asians for 5 percent.[252]

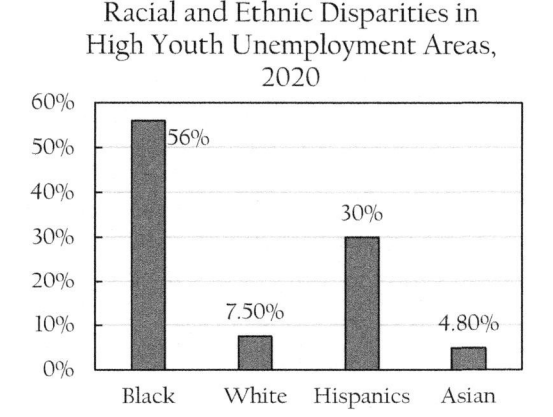

Racial and Ethnic Disparities in High Youth Unemployment Areas, 2020

Group	Unemployed Youth in PUMAs with high youth unemployment
Black	56%
White	7.50%
Hispanics	30%
Asian	4.80%

Figure 8.4. Source: Federal Reserve Bank of Chicago

Neighborhoods suffering from high youth unemployment and weaker overall labor market conditions are also notable for differences in racial demographics.[253] In areas with high youth unemployment, 45 percent of the population is Black, 33 percent is Hispanic, and only 16 percent is non-Hispanic White.[254] The parts of Chicago with lower youth unemployment comprise 8 percent Black, 23 percent Hispanic, and 58 percent non-Hispanic White

---

[252] Engel, Emily; Keller, Jason; O'Dell, Mark. "A few Examples of Chicago Tackling Youth Joblessness." *ProfitWise News and Views*. No. 5. (2018). pp. 1-11. Federal Reserve of Chicago.
[253] Ibid. p. 3
[254] Ibid. p. 3

181

residents.[255] The lack of job prospects in neighborhoods with high youth unemployment rates is based on the poor quality of education in these neighborhoods. For the population age 19 to 24 in Chicago neighborhoods with high youth unemployment, 85 percent have at least a high school diploma.[256] In Chicago neighborhoods with low youth unemployment, that figure increases to 96 percent.[257] Strikingly, 81 percent of unemployed youth in areas with high youth unemployment have high school diplomas.[258] The problem is that most of those youngsters who have high school diplomas but jobless, are jobless because they pursued their education in neighborhoods where the quality of education was extremely poor. Public schools in Chicago are subsidized by the Chicago city government.

The subsidization of public schools already disincentivizes teachers from doing their best to ensure that students learn as much as possible to meet the national standards. These subsidies guarantee lifetime employment for these teachers, which lessens their inclination to do their best for these students. In addition, public schools in poor neighborhoods are much worse managed than public schools in more affluent neighborhoods because they assume that these children have no future. Thus, these children from disadvantaged neighborhoods see no value in pursuing higher education and therefore indulge in all kinds of counterproductive

---

[255] Ibid. p. 3
[256] Ibid. p. 3
[257] Ibid. p. 3
[258] Ibid. p. 3

habits that they believe will help them improve their lives. Consequently, crime increases faster in low-income neighborhoods than in affluent neighborhoods.

3. The Police and the Black Community

Relations between the police and the Black community are perhaps the most strained and contentious relations in the social and cultural history of the United States. Since the abolition of slavery, the Black community has always been suspicious of the police, and this sentiment of distrust is also reciprocated by the police towards the Black community.

Members of the Black community, especially those from low-income neighborhoods, see the police as the armed forces of institutional racism. For them, the predominantly White police force reflects the continuation of the oppressive system that was implemented to maintain Blacks and other minority groups as second-class citizens. They maintained that when the police stop them for basic routine checks, these street stops are based on the fact that the police correlated their skin color with their social status, i.e., since they are Black, it is therefore assumed that they are necessarily criminals or could be criminals. It ought to be said that this sentiment of distrust of the Black community towards the police is not unwarranted.

Indeed, it is not wrong to assert that racial prejudice remains a factor in the judgment of police officers, especially White police officers when performing routine checks on Blacks and Latinos. Unfortunately, racial prejudice is part of human nature as we all judge those who look different than us one way or another. However, does this mean that all White police officers who are policing in Black neighborhoods and perform routine checks on them are necessarily motivated by their racial prejudice? Certainly not. According to the U.S. Census Bureau, Whites have been killed by the police far more than Blacks and Hispanics between January 2015 and March 2021.

Fatal Police Shooting and Population Size by Ethnic Group

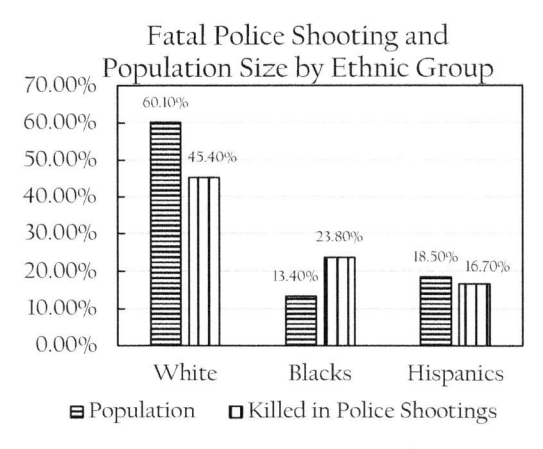

Ethnic Group	Population	Killed in Police Shootings
White	60.10%	45.40%
Blacks	13.40%	23.80%
Hispanics	18.50%	16.70%

Figure 8.5. Source: U.S. Census Bureau, Washington Post Police Shootings Database

Of course, this could be argued based on the population size. Whites are population-wise the largest community in the United States as they represent 60.1 percent of the national population but 45.4 percent within these 60.1 percent are killed by the police. Blacks represent 13.4 percent of the national population, and 23.8 percent within these 13.4 percent are killed by the police. This number though does not outpace the percentage of Whites that have been killed by the police between 2015 and 2021. Hispanics represent 18.5 percent of the national population and 16.7 percent within these 18.5 percent have been shot by the police. According to a 2020 Harvard study, Black Americans are 3.23 times more likely than White Americans to be killed by the police, but White Americans account for the highest percentage of people killed by the police in the United States. Another data from the Bureau of Justice Statistics exhibit the trend of police shootings by race. In these data, Whites also do represent a higher number of deaths by the police shootings than Blacks and other racial groups. Although the police may have some racial prejudice against Black people, which cannot be ruled out because we are all human beings and human beings are fallible beings, the evidence suggests otherwise that those police shootings are not intrinsically motivated by these racial prejudices because if race were the primary factor leading to police shootings, then White Americans would have had a significantly lower percentage of shootings than any other racial group.

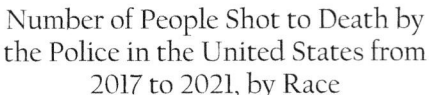

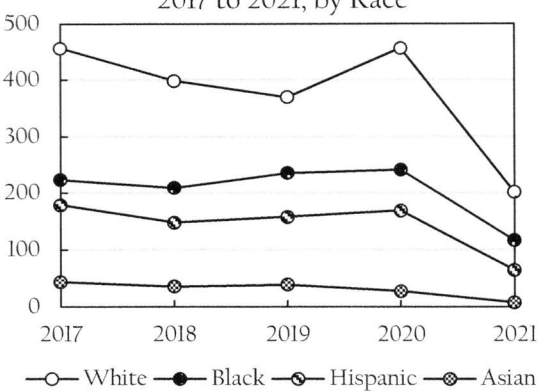

Number of People Shot to Death by the Police in the United States from 2017 to 2021, by Race

—○— White —●— Black —⊘— Hispanic —⊗— Asian

Figure 8.6. Source: Bureau of Justice Statistics

Blacks and Whites' views on police performance diverge greatly regarding the performance of the police between the police and Blacks. Blacks are clearly less confident than Whites in their local police. According to a 2016 study conducted by the Pew Research Center, only about slightly above one-third (36 percent) of the public claims they have a lot of confidence in their police department.[259] Confidence in local police has been considerably lower among Blacks, as just 14 percent say they have a lot of confidence in their local police, and 41 percent say they have some confidence.[260] Most Whites (75 percent) say their local police do an excellent or good

---

[259] Morin, Rich; Stepler, Renee. "The Racial Confidence Gap in Police Performance." *Pew Research Center.* (2016).
[260] Morin & Stepler, 2016

job when it comes to using the right amount of force for each situation.[261] Only 33 percent of Blacks share this view; 63 percent say the police do only a fair or poor job in this area.

Views on Police Performance by Race

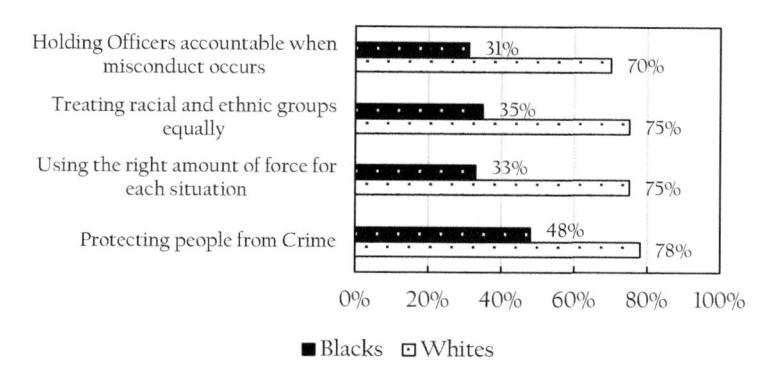

	Blacks	Whites
Holding Officers accountable when misconduct occurs	31%	70%
Treating racial and ethnic groups equally	35%	75%
Using the right amount of force for each situation	33%	75%
Protecting people from Crime	48%	78%

Figure 8.7. Source: Pew Research Center

During street checks in low-income neighborhoods, Blacks generally exhibit a recalcitrant attitude towards commands from the police, which prompts police officers to resort to the use of physical force which is considered a blunder. US police forces are trained to use force if the suspect displays a belligerent attitude that puts the officer's life in imminent danger. On the other hand, for Blacks who practice hood culture, resisting the police is seen as an act of bravery against the oppressor. The more a Black suspect resists the commands of the police officer, the more this suspect demonstrates his disobedience to authority and the rule of law. The primary role of the

---

[261] Morin & Stepler, 2016

police is to enforce the rule of law in the streets and resisting arrest is perceived as a challenge to the rule of law. In the United States, the rule of law trumps everything and any individual who decides to challenge the rule of law by displaying a belligerent or a recalcitrant behavior is considered a non-law-abiding citizen and therefore a danger to society that must be neutralized before it causes more harm. The following data show the percentage of residents who agree or strongly agree with each statement on the perception of police bias.

Perceptions of Police Bias

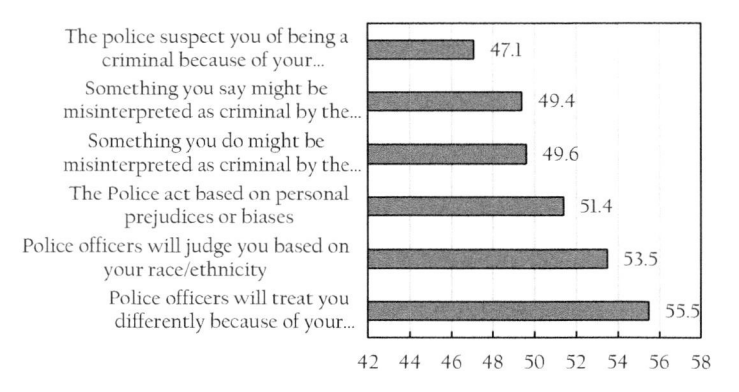

Statement	%
The police suspect you of being a criminal because of your...	47.1
Something you say might be misinterpreted as criminal by the...	49.4
Something you do might be misinterpreted as criminal by the...	49.6
The Police act based on personal prejudices or biases	51.4
Police officers will judge you based on your race/ethnicity	53.5
Police officers will treat you differently because of your...	55.5

Percentage of residents who agree or strongly agree with each statement

Figure 8.8. Source: Urban Analysis of Surveys of Residents in Birmingham, AL; Fort Worth, TX; Gary, IN; Minneapolis, MN; Pittsburgh, PA and Stockton, CA.

Community policing relies on collaboration among residents, businesses, and other local stakeholders to engage in proactive strategies that prevent crime and social disorder and support healthy and safe communities. In low-income Black neighborhoods, this collaboration is quasi non-existent. In affluent Black neighborhoods, however, a collaboration between the police and residents is well-established. For example, in an article published by Ronald Weitzer in the *Law and Society Review* (2000), the results of his empirical research suggest that Blacks living in affluent neighborhoods and Blacks living in low-income neighborhoods do not receive the same treatment.[262] The study focused on Washington, D.C. where three neighborhoods were examined: a middle-class White neighborhood, a middle-class Black neighborhood, and a lower-class Black neighborhood. These neighborhoods are Cloverdale (middle-class White neighborhood), Merrifield (middle-class Black neighborhood), and Spartanburg (lower-class Black neighborhood).[263] Merrifield residents asserted that they received similar treatment as White neighborhoods, while Spartanburg residents overwhelmingly characterized their neighborhood as receiving inferior treatment. Merrifield's socioeconomic status manifests itself in well-maintained houses and yards and an absence of signs of neighborhood disorder: there are no abandoned houses, no open-air drug markets, and few young people loitering in public places and causing trouble.[264] Logically, crime is much lower in such a neighborhood like Merrifield, therefore, the need for constant policing is not a necessity. In Spartanburg, however, crime rate is much higher, groups of idle young

---

[262] Weitzer, Ronald. "Racialized Policing: Residents' Perceptions in Three Neighborhoods." *Law & Society Review.* Vol. 34, No. 1 (2000), pp. 129-155
[263] Ibid. p. 134
[264] Ibid. p. 151

people frequent the streets, crack houses exist, street corner drug selling is prevalent, and other street deviants (prostitutes, homeless) can be found.[265] Hence, based on how the lifestyle of Spartanburg is managed, police intervention would be more than ever needed to monitor safety than in a neighborhood like Merrifield.

We can see indeed that although racial biases exist within the police, the differential treatment between communities is not fundamentally based on race but the socioeconomic status of communities. In short, the higher is the socioeconomic status of a neighborhood, the less policing is required and the lower is the socioeconomic status of a neighborhood, the more policing is required.

Policing in Affluent Black Neighborhoods

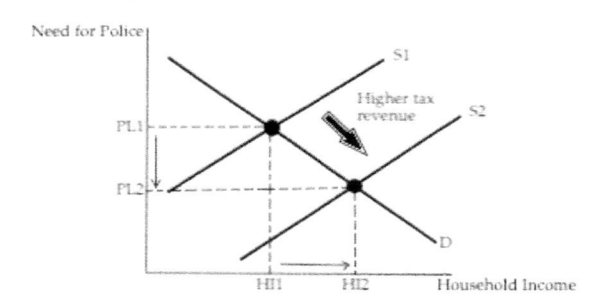

Figure 8.9.

---

[265] Ibid. p. 151

Policing in Low-Income Black Neighborhoods

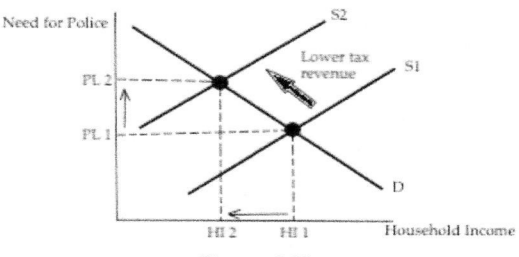

Figure 8.10.

Many studies suggest that Black Americans are disproportionately more incarcerated than any other racial and ethnic group. However, data from the Bureau of Justice Statistics (figure 8.11) suggest that White make up 57.7 percent of the inmate population while Blacks make up 38.3 percent of the inmate population. Nonetheless, Blacks do fill up jail cells at a faster rate than Whites and therefore increase prison populations. Figure 8.12 shows that Black Americans are incarcerated at 4.8 times the rate of White Americans.

Inmate Population by Race, 2022

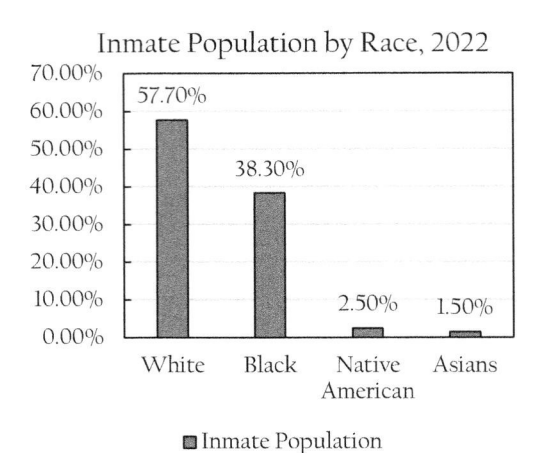

- White: 57.70%
- Black: 38.30%
- Native American: 2.50%
- Asians: 1.50%

Figure 8.11. Source: Bureau of Justice Statistics

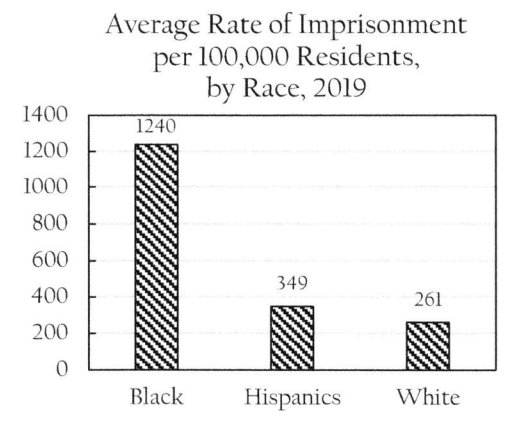

Average Rate of Imprisonment per 100,000 Residents, by Race, 2019

- Black: 1240
- Hispanics: 349
- White: 261

Figure 8.12. Source: Bureau of Justice Statistics, U.S. Census Bureau

The high rate of incarceration of Blacks in American prisons is a precursor to generational poverty. As was aforementioned in the previous chapters, prisons play a critical role in preventing Black Americans from escaping poverty. It is highly unlikely that a person who has been to prison, especially from a younger age, will create generational wealth for his descendants. On the contrary, generational poverty will be his lot because a former prisoner becomes socially handicapped and doomed to live in poverty for the rest of his life.

4. **Summary**

The youth represent the future of a community. When left to its own devices, without a parental compass, it is highly likely to succumb to violence and criminality. Being involved in criminal activities increases the likelihood of one to either ending up in jail or being killed by the police. One ends up in jail will eventually live in poverty for the rest of his life.

The Black community has developed a strong suspicion toward law enforcement which has tensed the relationships between police officers and Black residents. Although police officers do exert racial bias in their judgment since they are human beings like all of us, the evidence suggests that the difference in treatment of racial groups is primarily motivated by the socioeconomic status of each ethnic group. Asian and Indian American households receive far less policing than Black Americans because these communities are in the highest percentiles of the income distribution while most Black American households are in the lowest percentiles of the income distribution. If Black American households earned the same kind of income as the Asian and Indian American households, then the police would treat the Black community differently and much better than it does right now. And the evidence clearly pointed out that Blacks from different social classes were treated differently by the police. Middle and upper-class Blacks are treated less condescendingly by the police than lower-class Blacks.

Hood culture does not work in favor of lower-class Blacks. But the problem is that Blacks have embraced hood culture as their own culture. Since hood culture is a rebellious and belligerent culture that rejects and denies authority, and rather promotes crime and violence, the police then react very defensively towards Blacks who seem in appearance to be criminals. This means Blacks who wear a certain type of attire that would make them look suspicious and like criminals such as wearing pants below their bottom, wearing a hoodie, and exhibiting their tattoos all over their body. Such a way to present oneself prompts the racial bias of White police officers to seek out to treat Blacks, especially those living in low-income neighborhoods, with contempt. In a survey published by the Public Policy Institute of California on police treatment of different racial groups, 44 percent of Asian Americans claimed that police treat ethnic groups equally most of the time while 22 percent of Asian Americans agreed that the police treat ethnic groups equally almost always. Blacks, naturally, differed sharply from other views of police as the data can show these views in figure 8.13.

Overall, hood culture increases the likelihood of a Black person being targeted by the police. This is something that could possibly change. Not right away because hearts and minds do not change that easily. Racial bias will unfortunately always exist. We believe that what the police respect in this country is one having an economic powerbase. As we know, Asian and Indian Americans are treated less contemptuously by the police than Blacks are because they have an economic powerbase. Until Blacks forsake the habits of hood culture and unite to develop the infrastructures they need in order to create their economic powerbase, they will never earn the respect of the police nor that of the institutions in general. And the same contemptuous treatment that the police inflict on them will perpetuate.

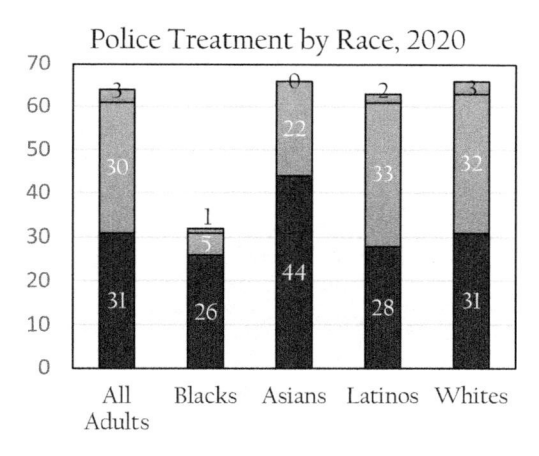

Police Treatment by Race, 2020

Group	Most of the time	Almost Always	Always
All Adults	31	30	3
Blacks	26	5	1
Asians	44	22	0
Latinos	28	33	2
Whites	31	32	3

■ Most of the time ▢ Almost Always ▢ Always

Figure 8.13. Source: PPIC Statewide Survey

9. PROPOSITIONS TO IMPROVE BLACK CULTURE

In American society, Black culture is synonymous with poverty because the Black community embraced hood culture as its own and made it the dominant culture of the community whereas hood culture is a culture inherently foreign to Black culture. Black culture is characteristically a conservative culture. Indeed, Black culture is a culture that has always been built on the respect for authority and hierarchy. The conservatism of Black culture is embedded in the respect for traditional values, the past, and the respect for authoritative figures. One of the main characteristics of Black culture is that it correlates authority with wisdom. It assumes that those who are in a position of authority are so because they have exhibited a set of moral principles and ethical values which promulgates that wisdom. Furthermore, Black culture is a culture that believes in the virtues of education and efforts in the expression of skills. And lastly, Black culture is a God-fearing culture.

As we can see, the basic characteristics of Black culture are not so different from the cultural characteristics of other racial minorities. They all believe in the same virtues (education, improvement of skills, individual efforts, merits...etc.) which are productive behaviors that lead to the development and fulfillment of man in a civilized society. This indicates in reality that, regardless of the cultural codes of an ethnic group, when the members of that group adopt productive behaviors, they inevitably become socioeconomically successful. And this has been countlessly proven over time.

As explained in chapter 4, the Black community, before the 1960s and the rise of the welfare state, was doing better economically and socially despite all the discriminatory laws that were put in place to prevent them from advancing. Most Black American families were nuclear families where 70 percent of children grew up in a two-parent household.[266] Their literacy rate increased dramatically in the 1930s and 1940s since, at the time, they valued education above all else. This does not mean that hood culture did not exist. On the contrary, it was already being practiced, but it was not as widespread as it is today.

Hood culture before the 1960s, occupied only a marginal position within the Black community. It was not until the implementation of the Civil Rights Act of 1964 that the hood culture began to gain more grounds and become more prevalent in Black culture. The prevalence of hood culture in the Black community is detrimental to its cultural identity. And this prevalence of hood culture in the Black community is the result of the counterproductive behaviors instigated by the aggrandizement of the welfare state. Today, hood culture is perceived as the cultural identity of the Black community. And this cultural identity is the engine of the perpetuation of generational poverty that increasingly stupefies the Black community. Nevertheless, since the Black community is not deterministic, it, therefore, has

---

[266] U.S. Bureau of the Census (1994)

the power to change its culture by rejecting the premises of hood culture and by reclaiming the conservative values that enabled it to be a community worthy and proud of its cultural roots. Hence, the main question to ask is to know how the Black community can improve its culture and the welfare of its community?

1. Self-Sufficiency Through Education and Skills Improvement

The pursuit of education is generally considered to be the surest path to rise in society. This is not an understatement, but a concrete statement. There is certainly a correlation between one's level of education and his income. Many studies have shown that the higher or more specialized is the education of an individual, the higher is the wage of that person. An individual who has pursued his education up to a certain level is more or less sure of being part of the middle-class. Indeed, 52 percent of the American population constitutes the middle class.[267] According to the Census data, anyone earning between $45,000 and $139,999 is considered middle-class, and according to the U.S. Bureau of Labor Statistics, an individual with a bachelor's degree earns an annual salary of $67,860 which puts that person in the middle-class and within the 50 percentile of the income distribution. In other words, a college degree suffices for an individual to be immediately middle-class and therefore avoid poverty. This is why Blacks need to

---

[267] Kochhar, Rakesh. "The American Middle Class is Stable in Size but Losing Ground Financially to Upper-Income Families." *Pew Research Center*. (2018)

prioritize education above all else as their primary path to escape poverty.

Household Income Range	Number of Households (Millions)	% of total	Notes
Less than $20,000	17.9	14%	Below or near poverty level
$20,000 to $44,999	26.5	20%	Low-Income
$45,000 to 139,999	68	52%	Middle-Class
$140,000 to $149,999	2.9	2%	Upper-Middle Class
$150,000 to $199,999	10.4	8%	High Income
$200,000+	13.3	10%	Highest tax brackets

Table 9.0. Source: U.S. Census Bureau

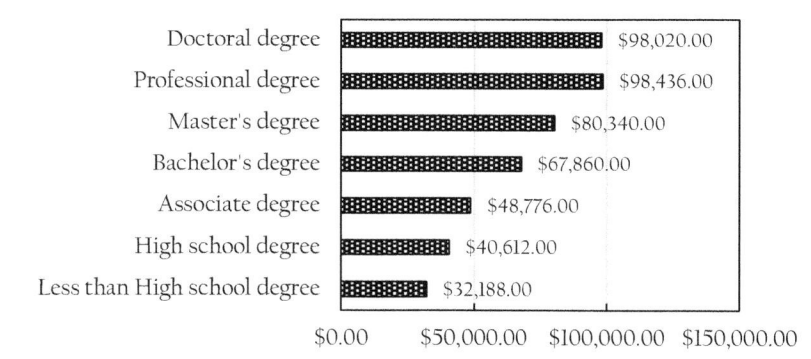

Median Income by Educational Attainment

Degree	Median Income
Doctoral degree	$98,020.00
Professional degree	$98,436.00
Master's degree	$80,340.00
Bachelor's degree	$67,860.00
Associate degree	$48,776.00
High school degree	$40,612.00
Less than High school degree	$32,188.00

Median Income by Educational Attainment

Figure 9.0. Source: U.S. Bureau of Labor Statistics

In the 1960s and 1970s, having a high school diploma sufficed to earn a comfortable living and be in the middle-class. Today, with technological progress that has changed the job market, having a post-secondary degree has become a necessity in order to obtain a job. It is, however, important for Blacks to be very selective in the academic subjects they want to study in their post-secondary studies because universities offer many degrees in several academic disciplines such as cultural studies, ethnic studies, gender studies, or ethnic studies. These academic disciplines are useless because they offer no practical skills relevant and useful to the demand of the labor market.

The principal reason why so many college graduates are unemployed is because they went into debt to earn useless degrees. With so much debt that ought to be paid, college graduates must perform low-skilled jobs that can barely make someone make ends meet. Blacks who aim to pursue their post-secondary education to the bachelor's level at the very least should study academic disciplines that offer practical, and job-ready skills such as STEMs (Science, Technology, Engineering, & Mathematics) or any other discipline that requires the use of quantitative reasoning such as Economics, Finance, or Accounting. Vocational education also remains a quintessential alternative to escape poverty because it provides practical skills that are ready to be used in the job market.

As a matter of fact, low-income individuals are poor not because they have a money issue, but because they have a skillset issue. And this lack of skills is what prevents them from obtaining high-paid jobs. Let us use a thought experiment to elucidate our point. Suppose two Black girls, Mary and Larissa, both 22 years old, just graduated college. Mary graduated with a degree in physics and a minor in mechanical engineering while Larissa graduated with a degree in African American Studies and a minor in philosophy. Let us assume that both girls have had internships during their college years, so they have acquired some work experience. Let us further assume that both girls have taken out student loans from the government to pay for their college education and they must obviously repay these loans to the government once they obtain a job. Six months later after graduating, Mary was hired as an entry-level engineering analyst by Lockheed Martin with a starting annual salary of $70,500. Though, the annual average salary of an entry-level job in America is roughly $40,000. Larissa, on the other hand, has been jobless. She cannot find a full-time job. She has been performing different jobs on a sporadic basis and yet, she still has her government loans to pay back. Based on her outstanding performances, Mary was promoted to higher responsibilities (associate engineering analyst) two years later with a new annual salary of $85,200 at age 24. Larissa, however, was able to find a job, and has been finally working full-time for a non-profit organization and earns an annual salary of $40,000 at age 24. As we can see, there is a difference of $45,200 between Mary and Larissa. Tired of earning a relatively low income, Larissa decides to enroll in a boot camp to learn how to program, with the hope of working as a software engineer. After completing the boot camp program in six months, Larissa was hired by a consulting firm as a software engineer with an annual salary of $71,000. With a higher salary, Larissa can now live more comfortably and no longer have to struggle to make ends meet.

The hypothetical scenario that we had just described indeed shows that Larissa had a skillset problem. Certainly, Larissa studied an academic discipline that the labor market did not find relevant. She selected a field of study without assessing her job prospects whereas Mary knew that if she studies physics and mechanical engineering, she will never be unemployed because people with either a physics, mathematics, computer science, or engineering degree are the most needed on the labor market. By switching to a more practical skillset such as software engineering, Larissa did not only solve her skillset problem, but she also elevated herself from one income bracket to another just by acquiring a new practical skillset. By acquiring a new skillset, she moved from the 31st percentile (lower-middle class) to the 53rd percentile (middle-class) of the income distribution. The Black community ought to focus on investing in their skillsets because skills are the foundation of a person's elevation in the socioeconomic ladder. A person with practical skills will inevitably avoid poverty and investing in practical skillsets will help the Black community avoid generational poverty.

2. Reduce Consumption and Increase Production

One of the major problems that keep the Black community in generational poverty is its consumption habits. Blacks spend more than produce and this creates a budget deficit in most Black households. As we have argued in previous chapters, the Black community spends a lot and spends mostly in depreciating rather than appreciative assets. And this type of investment limits the growth of money, which therefore prevents the creation of generational wealth.

It must be said that many Blacks start a lot of small businesses, but these small businesses have a hard time getting off the ground because their owners are spending the money which is supposed to be the capital meant to grow the business. The process of profitability of a company generally takes between three and five years. During this period, the owner of the business reinvests immediately the profit generated. However, the conundrum is that many owners do not reinvest the profit of their business and use it instead for personal purposes. But the worst part is that many small Black businesses are financially built on bank credit. When the owners, therefore, use the profit of their businesses for personal gain, they accumulate even more debt which they must repay to the bank and that is why many small Black businesses are not growing or simply go bankrupt. What then could be done to remedy this situation?

It is imperative for the Black community to change its habits by commencing to become more frugal. Frugality plays a foremost role in the creation of wealth. One of the reasons Jews are considered the wealthiest minority group in the world is because they are extremely frugal. To understand why Jewish people are so wealthy, it is because they have adopted a set of attitudes toward money, wealth, and poverty. In Jewish culture, avoiding poverty is a cultural obligation and a moral duty. Hence, to avoid poverty, Jewish people are exhorted to earn their living through gainful employment.[268] Jewish law calls upon Jews to do everything in their power to avoid becoming a burden to others.[269] They are responsible for their own welfare and not to rely on the community for them.[270] Poverty is a moral and cultural dishonor for Jews. Being poor in the Jewish community demonstrates one's inability to become self-sufficient, thus becoming a burden for others. This is why Jewish people, in addition to occupying high-paid jobs, are very frugal in their spending habits.

Being frugal allows one to save considerable sums of money and invest these sums in appreciative assets. But being frugal requires an enormous financial refrain from spending, a refrain that is critically lacking in the Black community. It is impossible to create generational wealth without being frugal.

Blacks could learn from Jews why poverty is something that no one shall be proud of. Blacks should change their mindset by rejecting poverty and make that rejection a cultural and moral imperative. So long as Blacks will continue to spend more than they produce, they will continue to be poor because no one can spend their way out of poverty. One does not become self-sufficient by spending more. One only becomes self-sufficient by saving more and investing more. Saving more means consuming less.

---

[268] Lifshitz, Joseph Isaac. *Markets, Morals, & Religion.* (2008). Transaction Publishers. p. 123
[269] Ibid. p. 123
[270] Ibid. p. 123

3. Make the Black Economy more Efficient

The Black community likes to boast itself by asseverating that it creates businesses. This is true. Black people do create a lot of businesses. But are all these Black-owned businesses profitable and sustainable? The predicament is that members of the Black community do not support each other, financially speaking. Black-owned businesses remain fragile because the circulation of the dollar in the Black community is inconsistent. This inconsistency of the circulation of the dollar distorts the allocation of resources within the Black community because Black businesses are created primarily to provide solutions specific to the Black community. This distortion creates a surplus of supply in the economy of the Black community. Black businesses produce, but Black consumers consume in lower quantity Black supplies.

Black-owned businesses produce goods and services primarily and mainly for Black consumers, but Black consumers do not spend enough on Black-owned businesses. The common recurring statistics in money circulation with communities, according to the NAACP, and other organizations, suggests that the Black dollar is unregulated.[271] Studies say that the average lifespan of the dollar is approximately 28 days in Asian communities, 19 days in Jewish communities, 17 days in White communities, and only 6 hours in Black communities.[272] Yet, the national buying power of Blacks in 2019 was $1.4 trillion but only 2 percent of that buying power is

---

[271] Marshall, Kamryn. "The Black Dollar Doesn't Circulate Like It Should." *The Famuan.* (2020).
[272] Marshall, 2020

recirculating in the Black community, according to a report by Selig Center for Economic Growth.[273] This suggests, indeed, Blacks have considerable purchasing power but do not use this purchasing power to enhance the profitability of Black-owned businesses, but rather enhance the profitability of multi-million-dollar corporations owned by White, Asians, and Jews. And this is a real problem. The enlargement of the racial wealth gap is partly due to this inconsistency of the circulation of the dollar in Black communities.

Blacks must realize that it is essential to keep the circulation of the dollar longer within the Black community before this money gets spent in other communities. Buying Black-owned products and services is one of the simplest ways to continue circulation.[274] More importantly, Black-owned businesses ought to refine their business model and expand their consumption targets. As was aforementioned, Black-owned businesses primarily focus on Black consumers, but Black consumers only represent 13 percent of the national population, which is clearly not much for scalability purposes. Black-owned businesses ought to expand their consumer-base demographics to other communities, especially White communities because they are the majority (population-wise) and have a higher purchasing power.[275] Let us use a hypothetical example to illustrate our point.

---

[273] Marshall, 2020
[274] Marshall, 2020
[275] Whites have a purchasing power of $12.5 trillion according to the Selig Center for Economic Growth, Terry College of Business at the

Let us assume that a Black barbershop has been operating in a middle-class Black neighborhood. This barbershop has been operating for a couple of years and only offered its services to Black consumers and its revenues were roughly about $328,000 a year. The owner of the barbershop, who is a Black man, decides to expand his services to Whites as well. Hence, he decided to hire four additional barbers, two Whites, and two Blacks. The Whites will be trained to cut Black people's hair in addition to cutting White people's hair, and the Blacks will be trained to cut White people's hair, in addition to cutting Black people's hair. As a result, the barbershop began to have a higher number of White customers while the number of Black customers remains constant. Consequently, the revenues of the barbershop tripled from $328,000 to $984,000 a year.

One of the reasons why companies such as Amazon, Apple, or Nike are extremely successful is because they did not limit their customer base to a certain demographics. When Jeff Bezos designed Amazon in his business model, he did not limit the supply of his services to Whites. He designed a business that would serve everyone regardless of their skin color, gender, or religious background. As a result, Amazon is one of the most profitable businesses in the history of entrepreneurship. Black-owned businesses should consequently adjust their business models to incorporate other demographics into their customer base. This adjustment will increase the profitability of Black-owned

---

University of Georgia, "The Multicultural Economy 2018," March 21, 2019.

businesses, which will subsequently improve the Black economy and will make it more efficient, hence improving the living standards of low-income Blacks, and offering them more economic opportunities.

10. WEALTH CREATION IN THE BLACK COMMUNITY

One of the greatest fallacies ever made in human history was to make people believe that the rich are despicable and greedy people whereas the poor are innocent people full of virtues. Striving for wealth is seen as a sin deserving the death penalty while being poor is now seen as a sign of humility. This dogma has been inculcated by Marxist writings into the subconscious of the collective mind. The belief that the rich are getting richer, and the poor are getting poorer because the rich exploit the poor is a nonsensical argument based on economic illiteracy. Anyone who has studied or read economics knows that the creation of wealth does not occur through the exploitation of the rich against the poor but rather through the supply of a service that responds to a particular demand. As French economist and philosopher, Jean-Baptiste Say asseverated in his 1803 book *Treatise on Political Economy*, "supply creates its own demand."

1. The Difference Between Rich and Poor

a) Rich and Poor's Attitudes Towards Money

The poor are no more virtuous than the rich. The fundamental difference between the rich and the poor is their attitude toward money. A rich person who consumes more than he saves and invests will eventually become poorer and a poor person who saves and invests more than he consumes will ultimately become richer. It is a matter of attitude.

Wealthy people are generally frugal while poor people are over-consumers. Poor people make decisions based on price while wealthy people make decisions based on the quality of their purchase. Thus, poor people always strive to buy the cheapest thing available in the market whereas the wealthy buy whatever they believe will produce the best return on their investment. As a result, since the poor focus more on price than quality, they end up purchasing the same commodity over and over, which leads to a lower return on their investment. If the cost exceeds its value, then this is clearly a loss on the return on investment.

For example, let us assume that two individuals, Michael and Andrew, each have $2,000. They both decided to purchase a laptop. Michael decided to purchase a refurbished computer online because it is cheaper. He bought his computer for $500. Andrew, on the other hand, decided to purchase a brand-new computer at the tech store for $1,500 with a warranty of $100 for a two-year time period, and other additional equipment the laptop needs ($200). Six months after the purchase, Michael's computer began to be defective while Andrew's computer works perfectly fine. Consequently, Michael decided to take his computer to the repairer and paid $400 in repair costs. Despite spending these $400 on repair costs, the functioning of his laptop did not improve. Michael was then forced to buy a new computer only six months after buying the previous laptop. This time, he spent $2,000 on a brand-new computer and bought all the equipment he needs this time to ensure that he will not have to spend any penny again on it. Andrew's computer, on the other hand, is still working flawlessly.

We clearly see that Michael based his initial decision on the price rather than the quality of the item. As a result, he ended up spending more than he initially thought he would. He spent $2,900 on a computer whilst Andrew only spent $1,800 on a one-time computer purchase. If Michael made the exact same choice as Andrew, he would have saved $1,100. Andrew invested in a computer that would last him at least a couple of years before the first defects start appearing while Michael invested in a cheap low-quality computer that only lasted him a couple of months. This example distinctly epitomized the difference between wealth and poverty's mindsets.

The attitude of Michael was not based on frugality at all. Michael was simply being avaricious. The main characteristic of frugality is based on necessary expenditures. A frugal person is someone who will never spend money on something he does not need. Frugal people spend money on things they believe are necessary and valuable in the long-run. Frugal people think like investors. Their spending is limited only to things that they consider necessary and whose value will appreciate over time. An avaricious attitude is an attitude where the person only cares about the fact that the price of a given item is cheap regardless of its quality. Avaricious people think that spending on expensive high-quality goods or services makes them lose money because they do not prioritize the value they will get from their purchase, but only the cost they will have to bear from it during the transaction process, which is, of course, a very short process. This again demonstrates that poor people do not think long-term but only short-term. As it is claimed that patience is a virtue, can we then say that the poor are virtuous people? If patience is a virtue, then it is a virtue that the poor are crucially lacking yet it is a virtue required in order to be lifted out of poverty.

b) *Blacks Attitude Towards Poverty*

Most members of the Black community support the Democratic Party and left-wing ideologies that promote social justice, government intervention in the economy to enforce more egalitarian policies, which they presumably believe, work in favor of the poor and the disadvantaged. For how long has the federal government been intervening in the economy to make things fairer for everyone, especially for Blacks? Since the 1960s, the federal government has been actively involved in implementing a series of egalitarian policies to help the Black community move upward socioeconomically.

Did the egalitarian policies enacted by the federal government make Black people much richer? Some may respond by the affirmative. If so, then why is the Black community still the poorest? Why does the Black community have a much lower household income than other communities? Blacks in favor of government intervention argue that the long-lasting poverty-stricken that is entrenched in the Black community is because of institutional racism. Yet, they want these institutions, which they claim to be racist, to help them create wealth through more egalitarian policies. The reality though is that no community in modern times became wealthier by using the law and the political process, especially laws that enhance egalitarian policies. Communities that became wealthier did so by using market mechanisms.

It is undeniable that poverty is part of the human condition, but it is not a fatality in itself. As a matter of fact, poverty has always been the starting point. The problem with the Black community's attitude towards poverty is that they have accepted it as a fatality, which consequently led them to embrace the victimhood mentality. As was aforementioned in the previous chapter, the Jewish community rejects poverty while the Black culture embraces it and subsequently expects exogenous resources (government and other communities) to help them solve their socioeconomic conundrums rather than relying on its endogenous resources to help themselves. This dependency on others has been a major drawback in Blacks' ability to generate wealth. The poverty-stricken problem in Black culture is not an exogenous problem but an endogenous one. Only Black people can solve their own problems; neither the government nor other communities can solve their problems for them.

2. The Evolution of the Creation of Wealth

a) *Wealth Creation in Pre-Capitalist Societies*

Before the growth of capitalism, wealth was created through the acquisition of land after wars were fought. The vanquished of the war had to concede their possessions to the victors, and in medieval times and even earlier than that, the acquisition of capital was defined by the possession of the land. The more lands one possesses, the richer he becomes.

Ownership of land was indispensable because the societies that predated capitalism were agrarian. The acquisition of capital in agrarian and pre-capitalist societies was done by force rather than by means of voluntary exchanges. Hence, access to capital was far more restricted than it was during the nineteenth century and beyond.

The acquisition of capital in pre-capitalist societies was done by law but these laws were certainly neither egalitarian nor libertarian. These laws were simply restrictive and greatly unfair, strictly designed for an elitist few. Pre-capitalist societies were very hierarchical where the Clergy occupied the top of this hierarchy, then the feudal lords, who were mainly landlords, formed the aristocratic class which owned capital. The peculiarity of this system is that the Clergy wrote their laws which allowed the landlords to access capital on the condition that they support the policy of the Clergy in return.[276] In short, the acquisition of capital was done by decree rather than by the laws of supply and demand.

Pre-capitalist societies were societies where upward economic mobility was static since access to capital and the accumulation of wealth were decreed by law. Those of the lower social classes could, therefore, never have

---

[276] Wood Meikskins, Ellen. *The Origin of Capitalism*. Verso, (2017). ISBN: 978-1786630681

access to capital. They were doomed to remain poor no matter how much they produce.

b) Wealth Creation in Capitalist Societies

The development of capitalism took shape with the expansion of the Industrial Revolution across Europe and in the United States, and the growth of the manufacturing sector. Capitalism, as an economic system, is mainly based on a dynamic system between production and consumption. Unlike pre-capitalist societies where access to capital and the creation of wealth were decreed by law, access to capital and the creation of wealth in capitalist societies have always been based on the laws of supply and demand. In capitalism, he who produces the most earns the most.

The capitalist system is an egalitarian and libertarian system. The word "egalitarian" will certainly shock more than one, and we expect it so. By affirming that the capitalist system is an egalitarian system, we imply that in such a system, individuals are all equal in terms of access to opportunities. Some will logically argue that this statement is fallacious because people do not have access to the same opportunities. Indeed, this is true. People do not have access to the same opportunities. But what they will fail to grasp is that people do not need to have access to the same opportunities. It is quintessential to understand that not all opportunities are created equal. For example, Michael Jackson and Michael Jordan both had the opportunity to play professional basketball. No law was created to prevent Michael Jackson from becoming an NBA player. The reason why Michael Jackson never became an NBA player is because he did neither have the skills nor the interest to become a professional basketball player. Just like Michael Jordan who never became a musical artist because he has neither the skills nor the interest to become a musical artist and yet he had the opportunity to venture into that field if he wanted to. Michael Jackson and Michael Jordan both became wealthy because they used their skills in their respective field of interest to produce something that consumers believed to be valuable. Capitalism is a libertarian system, on the other hand, because individuals are free to use their resources the way they see fit. There is no law commanding how one ought to use his resources. Capitalism is a free system of production based on voluntary exchange.

Since the capitalist system is a dynamic system, then upward economic mobility is easily ascertained. Access to capital is not restricted by law like in pre-capitalist societies. The capitalist system allows the poorest to have access to economic mobility because an individual who has an idea can materialize it. The capitalist system encourages the materialization of ideas, and the materialization of ideas creates entrepreneurs. This is why, unlike pre-capitalist societies where only aristocrats and the Clergy held access to capital, entrepreneurs are the ones who hold access to capital in capitalist societies. The interesting fact about entrepreneurship is that it is not a restricted domain. It is, on the contrary, a wide-open domain where everyone is welcome to venture in but not everyone is granted to be successful because entrepreneurship is a challenging, demanding, yet rewarding endeavor that requires a lot of personal sacrifices.

Entrepreneurs are the "aristocrats" of the capitalist system, but their "aristocracy" is based on meritocracy rather than being decreed by law. Entrepreneurs are ordinary people who most lifted themselves out of poverty by creating and offering a product or service to the market that consumers find valuable. Entrepreneurs take a huge risk when venturing into starting a new business. There is no guarantee that their business venture will be a success. That is why when their business venture becomes successful, they subsequently become wealthy.

A good example of a success story is Sam Walton, the owner and founder of Walmart, who started from very humble beginnings and yet become at some point, the wealthiest man in the United States. He created a retail empire that expanded across the country. He developed, perhaps, one of the simplest business models ever in which he would sell basic consumer goods at a very low price. This strategy ousted his competitors and increased consumer demands for basic necessities that they can afford at a low price. Interestingly, Jeff Bezos, the founder and owner of Amazon, Inc. used the Sam Walton strategy of selling goods at a lower price than his competitors. The result has been the same as Sam Walton, Jeff Bezos became one of the wealthiest men alive in the United States and the world today.

3. Generational Wealth in the Black Community

Why is the creation of generational wealth a problem in the Black community? It is a problem because the Black nuclear family has been decimated by welfare policies.

The purpose of creating generational wealth is to pass down the wealth created to the next generations.

The White community no longer reproduces as it used to. It is in decline, yet wealth continues to be produced abundantly in this community. Where will this wealth go if there is a reproduction deficit? The following data show statistically the decline of births and the rise of deaths of the White population in the United States. In the early 2000s, the White population represented 75 percent of the national population. By 2020, this rate has declined to roughly 60 percent.[277] White women have an average of 1.7 children over their lifetimes, while Hispanic women average 2.2.[278] The total fertility rates of Blacks, Asians, and Amerindians are in between.[279] So Whites have fewer births than all non-White groups.[280] Blacks make more children and yet produce less wealth than Whites.

---

[277] Poston, Dudley L.; Bouvier, Leon F. *Population and Society: An Introduction to Demography.* (2016). ISBN: 978-110-764-5936
[278] Ibid.
[279] Ibid.
[280] Ibid.

Declining White Population
(in millions)

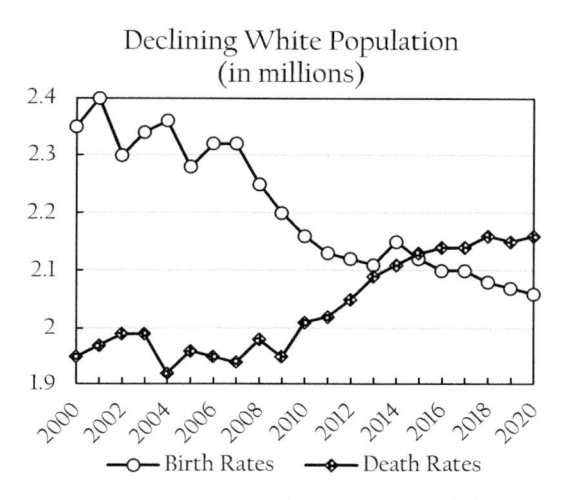

Figure 10.0. Source: National Center for Health Statistics

In order to create generational wealth to grow the Black economy, its members must change their mindset and adopt more productive behaviors. This change of mentality proceeds by a set of steps that ought to be applied:

- Rejecting poverty and hood culture behaviors;
- Rejecting the welfare state and its programs;
- Applying frugality to their finances;
- Investing in the education, and skills;
- Becoming self-reliant
- Increasing financial literacy, investing in the stock market and other appreciating assets;
- Developing infrastructures to make the Black economy more sustainable;

These steps lead to the creation of generational wealth. This is what other communities have done for the last two centuries or so in the United States in order to maintain long-term prosperity. If the Black community decides to value again the traditional values such as maintaining the nuclear family and teaching children the value of money, hard work, and the principles of a successful life in general, then the forthcoming generations of Black will undeniably be successful for several decades to come. Today, there is no law preventing Blacks from becoming successful. It is mainly a matter of changing behaviors.

Changing behaviors is not a deterministic process but a consequentialist one. Black people, like any other human being, are responsible for their actions. They can decide to escape poverty if they want to. Constantly blaming exogenous factors for endogenous problems when there is no longer any real obstacle to prevent them from advancing, is an old and outdated tactic to make excuses as to why things do not work out. Change is painful, but no gain could be obtained without pain. All the communities that are successful today are so because they have endured the pain of change before gaining success. Until the Black community becomes financially sustainable, it will never earn the respect of other communities as well as that of the police. The world in which we live is a ruthless world where only those with a strong economic powerbase are respected and considered. The Black community, for now, lacks this economic powerbase.

The respect and social acceptance to which the Black community aspires can never be achieved until it establishes an economic powerbase. This economic powerbase can only be ensconced and maintained through generational wealth. It is once generational wealth is well-entrenched in the Black community that they will finally start earning the respect of others. Until then, the police will continue to treat Black people with condescendence, and other communities will continue to think that Black people are eternal beggars. Political power will not make the Black community socioeconomically better-off, only self-reliance through a strong and well-established economic powerbase will.

REFERENCES

Introduction

1. *Oxford Dictionary*

2. Consequentialism is the doctrine that the morality of an action is to be judged solely by its consequences. Consequentialism argues that actions have consequences and the person who has initiated the act is therefore responsible for the consequences of that act initiated.

Chapter 1: How is Poverty Measured?

3. Federal income tax is 33% for individual making between $86,376 and $164,925 a year and California income tax is 9.3% for people making between $61,215 and $312,686 a year. (24% + 9.3% = 33.3%). Source: *U.S. Department of the Treasury.*

4. Cost of living includes housing cost, food cost, gas cost, taxes, healthcare, clothing, education, transportation, entertainment…etc.

5. Utah has a flat state income tax. Regardless of income bracket, every taxpayer living in Utah pays the same tax rate.

6. Rubenstein, Jennifer. "Pluralism and Global Poverty." *British Journal of Political Science.* Vol. 43, No. 4. (2013). pp. 775-797

7. DL = Demand for Labor; SL = Supply for Labor

8. Ibid.

9. Keister, Lisa A.; Moller, Stephanie. "Wealth Inequality in the United States." *Annual Review of Sociology,* Vol. 26. pp. 63-81.

10. Ibid. p. 63

11. Ibid. p. 63

12. Ibid. p. 63

13. Perry, Mark J. "Some Amazing Findings on Income Mobility in the U.S. including the Image of a Static 1 and 99 percent is False." *American Enterprise Institute.* (2017).

14. Perry, 2017

15. Perry, 2017

16. Sowell, Thomas. "Income Facts and Fallacies." *Economic Facts and Fallacies,* (2008). p. 138. Basic Books, New York. ISBN: 978-0-465-0-22-038.

17. Ibid. p. 138

18. Ibid. p. 146

19. Ibid. p. 146

20. Ibid. p. 146

21. Ibid. p. 146

22. Ibid. p. 146

23. Ibid. p. 147

24. Ibid. p. 147

25. Ringold, Dena; Orenstein, Mitchell A.; Wilkens, Erika. "Overview." *Roma in an Expanding Europe: Breaking the Poverty Cycle*, (2005). p. xiv. The World Bank. ISBN: 0-8213-5457-4

26. Ibid. p. xiv

27. Ibid. p. xiv

28. Ibid. p. xiv

29. Ibid. p. xiv

30. Ibid. p. xv

31. Ibid. p. xv

32. Ibid. p. xv

33. Staff, *80% of Roma are at Risk of Poverty, New Survey Finds*, European Union Agency for Fundamental Rights. (2016).

34. Staff, 2016

35. *How is Poverty Measured?* Institute for Research on Poverty. University of Wisconsin-Madison

36. Ibid.

37. Ibid.

38. Ibid.

39. Ibid.

40. Fox, Liana; Burns, Kalee. "The Supplemental Poverty Measure: 2020." *U.S. Census Bureau.* P-60-275. (2021). Pp. 1-37

Chapter 2: Racism & Generational Poverty

41. A Fascinating Map of the World's Most and Least Racially Tolerant Countries." *The Washington Post.* (2015). ISSN: 0190-8286.

42. Washington, Robert E. "Brown Racism and the Formation of a World System of Racial Stratification." *International Journal of Politics, Culture, and Society.* Vol. 4. No. 2. (1990). pp. 209-227

43. Jones, Terry. "Institutional Racism in the United States." *Social Work.* Vol. 19, No. 2. (1974). pp. 218-225

44. Ibid. p. 220

45. Ibid. p. 220

46. Ibid. p. 220

47. Ibid. p. 220

48. Meehan, Deborah. "Structural Racism and Leadership." *Race, Poverty & the Environment.* Vol. 17, No. 2. (2010), pp. 41-43

49. "Social Justice." *Oxford Languages.*

50. *What is Social Justice?* Pachamama Alliance (2019).

51. Novak, Michael. "Social Justice: Not What You Think It Is." *Heritage Lectures.* No. 1138. The Heritage Foundation. (2009).

52. Sightings, Tom. "7 Myths About Millionaires." *U.S. News.* (2018)

53. Blunden, G. H. "A Progressive Income Tax." *The Economic Journal.* Vol. 5, No. 20. (1895). pp. 527-531

54. Spalding, Matthew. "Why the U.S. has a Culture of Dependency." *Political Op-Ed.* Cable News Network. (2012).

55. "Affirmative Action" *Legal Information Institute.* Cornell Law School

56. Verbruggen, Robert. "Two Points about the Harvard Affirmative-Action Ruling." *National Review.* (2019)

57. Verbruggen, 2019

58. Avi-Yonah, Shera; McCafferty, Molly C. "Asian-American Harvard Admits Earned Highest Average SAT Score of Any Racial Group From 1995 to 2013." *The Harvard Crimson.* (2018)

59. Perry, Mark, J. "The Downside of Affirmative Action: Academic Mismatch." *American Enterprise Institute.* (2012)

60. Sander, Richard; Taylor, Stuart. "The Painful Truth About Affirmative Action." *The Atlantic.* (2012)

61. Sander & Taylor, 2012.

62. De Leon, Adrian. *The Long History of Racism Against Asian Americans in the U.S.* PBS. (2020)

63. De Leon, 2020

64. De Leon, 2020

65. *Asian Americans Then and Now,* Center for Global Education. Asia Society.

66. Ibid.

67. De Leon, 2020

68. De Leon, 2020

69. Harvard Law Review Association. "Racial Violence Against Asian Americans." *Harvard Law Review*. Vol. 106, No. 8. (1993), pp. 1926-1943

70. Ibid. p. 1931

71. Ibid. p. 1931

72. Ibid. p. 1931

73. Ibid. p. 1931

74. Badrinathan, Sumitra; Kapur, Devesh; Kay, Jonathan; Vaishnav, Milan. "Summary." *Social Realities of Indian Americans: Results from the 2020 Indian American Attitudes Survey*. (2020). Carnegie Endowment for International Peace. pp. 1-63

75. Ibid. p. 43

76. Ibid. p. 43

77. Ibid. p. 43

78. Ibid. p. 44

79. Joo, Nathan; Reeves, Richard V.; Rodrigue, Edward. "Asian-American Success and the Pitfalls of Generalization." *Brookings Institute.* (2016).
80. Ryan, Camille L.; Bauman, Kurt. "Educational Attainment in the United States: 2015." *Current Population Reports.* U.S. Department of Commerce—Economics and Statistics Administration. U.S. Census Bureau.

81. *Brookings Institute,* 2016

82. *Brookings Institute,* 2016

83. *Brookings Institute,* 2016

84. *Brookings Institute,* 2016

85. *Brookings Institute,* 2016

86. *Brookings Institute,* 2016

87. McNulty, Jennifer. "Success of Indians in the U.S. showcases Importance of Education." *Newscenter.* (2017). University of California, Santa Cruz

88. McNulty, 2017

89. McNulty, 2017

90. McNulty, 2017

91. McNulty, 2017

92. McNulty, 2017

Chapter 3: Black Culture and the Welfare State

93. Perazzo, John, "How The Liberal Welfare Destroyed Black America: What Democrat Voters And Political Leaders Refuse To Believe", *FrontPage Magazine.* (2016).

94. Perazzo, Ibid.

95. Perazzo, Ibid.

96. Perazzo, Ibid.

97. Rector, Robert; Menon, Vijay. "Understanding the Hidden $1.1 Trillion Welfare System and How to Reform It." *Backgrounder.* No. 3294. (2018). The Heritage Foundation.

98. Perazzo, Ibid.

99. Perazzo, Ibid.

100. Perazzo, Ibid.

101. Perazzo, Ibid.

102. Perazzo, Ibid.

103. Perazzo, Ibid.

104. Perazzo, Ibid.

105. Perazzo, Ibid.

106. Perazzo, *Ibid.*

107. Williams, Walter E., " The Welfare State's Legacy", *Creators Syndicate.* 2007

108. Philipps, Grants, "US History Shows The Minimum Wage Has Harmed The Black Community", *Panam Post.* (2016)

109. Phillips, Ibid.

110. Philipps, Ibid.

111. Philipps, Ibid.

112. Philipps, Ibid.

113. Philipps, Ibid.

114. William, E. Even, David A. Macpherson, "Unequal Harm: Racial Disparities Consequences of Minimum Wage Increases", *Employment Policies Institute.* (2011) Policy Research.

115. Garthwaite, Craig, "Minimum Increase Hurts Low-Income Families", *Employment Policies Institute.* (2005)

116. Poper, Rob, "High Minimum Wages Were Designed To Hurt Minorities", *Ethan Allen Institute.* (2018)

117. Poper, Ibid.

118. Poper, Ibid.

119. Poper, Ibid.

120. Perry, Mark, "Thomas Sowell on the differential impact of the minimum wage." *American Enterprise Institute.* (2016)

121. Perry, Ibid.

122. Tanner, Michael D., "Relationship Between The Welfare State and Crime." *Cato Institute.* (1995)

123. Tanner, Ibid.

124. Moore, Stephen, "Why Trump is better for Black America than Obama ever was." *The Hill.* (2017)

125. Mitchell, Daniel J. "Obama's Failure on Jobs: Four Damning Charts." *Forbes.* (2011)

Chapter 4: Black Culture & Counterproductive Habits

126. Paisley, Harris. "Gatekeeping and Remaking: The Politics of Respectability in African American Women's History and Black Feminism." *Journal of Women's History.* Vol.15. (2003) p. 213

127. Nuñez-Franklin, Brianna. Democracy Limited: The Politics of Respectability. *Democracy Limited: The Suffrage "Prison Special" Tour of 1919.*

128. Young, Jeremy C. "Booker T. Washington and the White Fear of Black Charisma." *Black Perspectives.* (2017)

129. Booker T. Gardner, "The Educational Contributions of Booker T. Washington." *Journal of the Negro Education.* Vol. 44, No. 4. (1975). pp. 502-518

130. Ibid. p. 506

131. Ibid. p. 506

132. Ibid. p. 506

133. Ibid. p. 507

134. Ibid. p. 507

135. Ibid. p. 507

136. We used a linear regression to test the correlation between the illiteracy rate of Blacks and their rate of employment in the agricultural sector. The model is the following: (Agriculture = β_0 + β_1IlliteracyRate + ε) We used the data from the U.S. Department of Commerce, U.S. Census Bureau, and the Historical Statistics of the United States. (n=18). The data was designed by decades until the year 1940

when it was spread every three or four years on average.

137. Bedell, Mary S. "Employment and Income of Negro Workers—1940-52." *Bureau of Labor Statistics.*

138. Cheeseman Day, Jennifer. "88% of Blacks Have High School Diploma, 26 % a Bachelor's Degree." *U.S. Census Bureau.* (2020).

139. Cheeseman Day, 2020

140. Sowell, Thomas. "Politics and Diversity." *Wealth, Poverty, and Politics.* (2016). p. 269. Basic Books. ISBN: 978-0465096763

141. Ibid. p. 269

142. Ibid. p. 269

143. Ibid. p. 269

144. Harris, Robert J. "Essay Review: On Thomas and African American Life and Culture." *The Journal of African American History.* Vol. 91. No. 3. (2006), pp. 328-334

145. *ZipRecruiter Data,* (2022)

146. The judicial average salary was calculated based on how much each federal judgeship makes annually.

147. Hypersexuality is an excessive preoccupation with sexual fantasies, urges, or behaviors that is difficult to control.

148. Schwab-Pomerantz, Carrie. *Does Marriage Bring Financial Benefits?* Charles Schwab. (2020)

149. *HIV and African American People*, CDC.

150. Ibid

151. Achinstein, Peter. "General Introduction." *Science Rules: A Historical Introduction to Scientific Methods.* John Hopkins University Press. (2004). ISBN: 0-8018-7943-4

152. Gauch, Hugh G. *Scientific Method in Practice.* Cambridge University Press. (2003). p. 45. ISBN: 978-0-521-01708-4

153. Lloyd, G.E.R. "The Development of Empirical Research," *Magic, Reason, and Experience: Studies in the Origin and Development of Greek Science.*

154. Ibid.

155. Sallam, Hassan. "Aristotle, Godfather of Evidence-Based Medicine." *Facts, Views & Vision in ObGyn.* Vol. 2, No. 1 (2010). pp. 11-19

Chapter 5: Black Culture, The Victimhood Mentality & Critical Race Theory

156. Borter, Gabriella. "Explainer: What Critical Race Theory means and Why It's Igniting Debate.?" *Reuters.* (2021).

157. Gillborn, David. "Intersectionality, Critical Race Theory, and the Primacy of Racism: Race, Class, Gender, and Disability in Education." *Qualitative Inquiry.* Vol. 21, No. 3. (2015). pp. 277-287

158. Crenshaw, Kimberle. "Mapping the Margins: Intersectionality, Identity Politics, and Violence Against Women of Color." *Stanford Law Review.* Vol. 43. No. 6. (1991). pp. 1241-1299

159. Ibid. p. 1266

160. Carbado, Devon W.; Gulati, Mitu. "The Law and Economics of Critical Race Theory." *The Yale Law Journal.* Vol. 112, No. 7. (2003). pp. 1757-1828

161. Ibid. p. 1758

162. Ibid. p. 1758

163. Ibid. p. 1758

164. Ibid. p. 1760

165. Ibid. p. 1760

166. Ibid. p. 1760

167. "How Groups Voted in 2008." *Roper Center for Public Opinion Research.* Cornell University

168. It is important to stress that the meaning of the word "liberal" has changed. In modern American political culture, a liberal is someone who supports a greater involvement of the government in economic and social affairs. An American liberal believes that it is the role of the government to intervene in the economy when the market fails or to regulate in order to tackle social issues. However, the original meaning of the word "liberal" suggests someone who believed in limited government, economic, political, and social freedom, and the rule of law. Original liberalism is known as *classical liberalism.*

Chapter 6: Black Culture & the Stock Market

169. Rent-seeking is the effort to increase one's share of existing wealth without creating new wealth. Rent-seeking results in reduced economic efficiency through misallocation of resources, reduced wealth creation, lost government revenue, heightened income inequality, and potential national decline.

170. United States Congress

171. "Census Bureau Release New Data on Minority-Owned, Veteran-Owned, and Women-Owned Business" *U.S. Census Bureau.* (2021).

172. Ibid.

173. "Interesting Facts & Statistics About Black-Owned Businesses." *The African American Business Guide.*

174. Baboolall, David; Cook, Kelemwork; Noel, Nick; Stewart, Shelley; Yancy, Nina. "Building Supportive Ecosystems for Black-Owned US Businesses." *McKinsey & Company.* (2020)

175. Ibid.

176. "The Racial Gap in Business Ownership Explained in Four Charts." *Aspen Institute.* (2017)

177. Aspen Institute, 2017

178. U.S. Census Bureau, (2020)

179. "Homeownership Rates Show That Black Americans are Currently The Least Likely Group to Own Homes." *USAFacts.* (2020)

180. Ibid.

181. Ibid.

182. Ibid.

183. Sowell, Thomas. "Bouncing Ball Politics." *Townhall.* (2013).

184. Sowell, 2013

185. Sowell, Thomas. "Urban Facts and Fallacies." *Economic Facts & Fallacies.* (2008). p. 25. Basic Books, New York. ISBN: 978-0-465-02203-8

186. Hendrix, Michael. "Rent Control Does Not Make Housing More Affordable." *Issue Brief.* Manhattan Institute. (2020).

187. Hendrix, 2020

188. Hendrix, 2020

189. Hendrix, 2020
190. Hendrix, 2020

191. Hendrix, 2020

192. Li, Yun. "Black Americans' Lack of Participation in the Stock Market Likely to Widen Post-Pandemic Wealth Gap." *CNBC.* (2022).

193. Li, 2022

194. Li, 2022

195. Li, 2022

196. Li, 2022

197. Choe, Stan. "Stocks are Soaring, and Most Black People are Missing Out." *ABC News.* (2020)

198. Choe, 2020

199. Choe, 2020

200. Choe, 2020

201. "Conspicuous Consumption and Race: Who Spends More on What." *Knowledge@Wharton.* The University of Pennsylvania.

202. Ibid.

203. Ibid.

204. Ibid.

205. Ibid.

206. Perkins, Erin C. *Tackling Disparities in Finance for Black and African Americans.* MonkeyGeek. (2022).

207. Yakoboski, Paul J. "Financial literacy, Wellness, and Resilience Among African Americans." *TIAA Institute-GFLEC Personal Finance Index.* (2020). pp. 1-23

208. Perkins, 2022

209. Perkins, 2022

210. TIAA Institute-GFLEC Personal Finance Index, 2020

211. We statistically tested the relationship between educational attainment for Blacks who have completed a college degree and Black households that own stocks. We initially intended to use the simple linear regression (SLR) to test this hypothesis. However, the lack of linearity prevented us from using the SLR. Hence, a linear regression would not fit in the data. Since the relationship between the dependent variable and predictor is not linear, we then used polynomial regression in order to capture all observations that are on the scatterplot. The statistical model can be denoted as $Y = \beta_0 + \beta_1 X_1 + \beta_2 X_1^2 + \beta_3 X_1^3 + \varepsilon$ where (Y), which is our dependent variable, represents the percentage of Black household owning stocks, and (X_1), which is our predictor, represents the percentage of Black Americans who completed a college degree. (X_1^2) and (X_1^3) are the new predictors added to the initial predictor. These predictors are simply the original predictor that has been extrapolated because the relationship between the dependent variable and the predictor is curvilinear. Lastly, (ε) represents the error term. The data used to test our hypotheses were mainly obtained from the Pew Research Center and the Federal Reserve Board. We built a cross-sectional dataset of 51 observations (n=51). After applying descriptive and inferential statistical methods, we found that the relationship between the two variables was statistically significant with a p-value significantly below 5% (p-value = 0.004). This,

henceforth, shows that there is sufficient evidence against the null hypothesis.

Chapter 7: Black Culture & Infrastructures

212. Puentes, Robert. "Why Infrastructure Matters: Rotten Roads, Bum Economy." *Brookings Institute.* (2015).

213. Puentes, 2015

214. President Biden. "Fact Sheet: Biden-Harris Administration Announces New Actions to Build Black Wealth and Narrow the Racial Wealth Gap." *Statements and Releases.* (2021). The White House.

215. De Rugy, Veronique. *Subsidies Are the Problem, Not the Solution, for Innovation in Energy.* (2015). Mercatus Center—George Mason University. pp. 1-5

216. Ibid. p. 2

217. Ibid. p. 2

218. Ibid. p. 2

219. Ibid. p. 2

220. Ibid. p. 2

221. Ibid. p. 3

222. Ibid. p. 3

223. Ibid. p. 3

224. Ibid. p. 4

225. Ibid. p. 4

226. Ibid. p. 4

227. Chatelain, Marcia. "The Burning House." *The Nation.* (2020).
228. Taylor, Keeanga-Yamahtta. *Race for Profit: How Banks and the Real Estate Industry Undermined Black Homeownership (Justice, Power, and Politics)*. University of North Carolina Press. (2019). ISBN: 978-1469653679

229. Chatelain, 2020

230. Perry, Andre M.; Boyea-Robinson, Tynesia; Romer, Carl. "How Black-owned businesses can make the most out of the Biden infrastructure plan?" *Brookings Institute.* (2021).

231. Friedman, Milton. "The Role of Monetary Policy." *The American Economic Review.* Vol. 58, No. 1. (1968). pp. 1-17

232. Ibid. p. 1

233. Dugyala, Rishika "US Banks teach financial literacy with Hands-on Experience." *Reuters.* (2018)

234. Dugyala, 2018

235. Neal, Michael; Walsh, John. *The Potential and Limits of Black-Owned Banks.* Urban Institute. (2020), pp. 1-16

236. Ibid. p. 2

Chapter 8: Black Culture, Crime, & Generational Poverty

237. "2019 Crime in the United States," *Federal Bureau of Investigation.* (2019).

238. Ibid.

239. Ibid.

240. Sowell, Thomas. "Black Redneck and White Liberals." *Black Rednecks and White Liberals.* (2005). p. 7. Basic Books, New York. ISBN: 978-1594031434

241. Ibid. p. 7

242. Ibid. p. 7

243. Dyson. R.W. "Nature, Morality and Realism: The Political Philosophy of Thomas Hobbes" *Natural Law and Political Realism in the History of Political Thought: Volume II—From the Seventeenth to the Twenty-First*

Century. (2007). p. 1-35. Peter Lang Publishing, New York. ISBN: 978-0820488820

244. Ibid. p. 15

245. Sweeny, Annie; Fry, Paige. "Nearly 33,000 juveniles arrested over last two decades labeled as gang members by Chicago Police." *Chicago Tribune* (2018).

246. Hagedorn, John; Aspholm, Roberto; Cordova, Teresa; Papachristos, Andrew; Williams, Lance. *Fracturing of Gangs and Violence: A Research-Based Reorientation of Violence Prevention and Intervention Policy.* Great Cities Institute University of Illinois at Chicago. (2019). pp. 1-28

247. Ibid. p. 7

248. Ibid. p. 8

249. Ibid. p. 8

250. Ibid. p. 8

251. We used the linear regression to test our hypothesis. The model could be denoted as: **Crime** = $\beta_0 + \beta_1 \text{YUEMP} + \varepsilon$ where Crime is our dependent variable, and (YUEMP), which is the predictor, represents the youth employment rate. Youth unemployment takes into account people between 16 and 24 years old. Our data contains 77 observations

(n=77). Each observation represents a neighborhood in the City of Chicago. The data were extracted from Chicago Data Portal and the Chicago Police Department. In assessing the descriptive statistics of the data, we saw that both variables (dependent and predictor) were extremely skewed. To avoid any potential misleading results, we applied the logarithm transformation to ensure that the values of both variables would fit in the data. The result of our regression suggests that the relationship between youth unemployment and crime in the city of Chicago is statistically very significant ($p < 0.001$) ($p = 1.0063 \times 10^{-9}$). Although there is a moderately strong correlation between the predictor and the dependent variable ($R = 0.627$), the proportion of the variance in the response variable that can be explained by the predictor is only 39.39% ($R^2 = 0.3939$). In other words, 39.39% of the variation in crime rate can be explained by the rate of youth unemployment.

252. Engel, Emily; Keller, Jason; O'Dell, Mark. "A few Examples of Chicago Tackling Youth Joblessness." *ProfitWise News and Views.* No. 5. (2018). pp. 1-11. Federal Reserve of Chicago.

253. Ibid. p. 3

254. Ibid. p. 3

255. Ibid. p. 3

256. Ibid. p. 3

257. Ibid. p. 3

258. Ibid. p. 3

259. Morin, Rich; Stepler, Renee. "The Racial Confidence Gap in Police Performance." *Pew Research Center.* (2016).

260. Morin & Stepler, 2016

261. Morin & Stepler, 2016

262. Weitzer, Ronald. "Racialized Policing: Residents' Perceptions in Three Neighborhoods." *Law & Society Review.* Vol. 34, No. 1 (2000), pp. 129-155

263. Ibid. p. 134

264. Ibid. p. 151

265. Ibid. p. 151

Chapter 9: Propositions to Improve Black Culture

266. U.S. Bureau of the Census (1994)

267. Kochhar, Rakesh. "The American Middle Class is Stable in Size but Losing Ground Financially to Upper-Income Families." *Pew Research Center.* (2018)

268. Lifshitz, Joseph Isaac. *Markets, Morals, & Religion.* (2008). Transaction Publishers. p. 123

269. Ibid. p. 123

270. Ibid. p. 123

271. Marshall, Kamryn. "The Black Dollar Doesn't Circulate Like It Should." *The Famuan.* (2020).

272. Marshall, 2020

273. Marshall, 2020

274. Marshall, 2020

275. Whites have a purchasing power of $12.5 trillion according to the Selig Center for Economic Growth, Terry College of Business at the University of Georgia, "The Multicultural Economy 2018," March 21, 2019.

Chapter 10: Wealth Creation in the Black Community

276. Wood Meikskins, Ellen. *The Origin of Capitalism.* Verso, (2017). ISBN: 978-1786630681

277. Poston, Dudley L.; Bouvier, Leon F. *Population and Society: An Introduction to Demography.* (2016). ISBN: 978-110-764-5936

278. Ibid.

279. Ibid.

280. Ibid.

LIST OF FIGURES & TABLES

Figures

1.0. Poverty Rate in the United States Before and After COVID

1.1. Unemployment Rate Post-CVOID

1.2. Lawyer's wife impact if employed after 5 years of inactivity in the labor market

1.3. Lawyer's impact on the labor market after 1 year of practicing law

1.4. U.S. Poverty Statistics by Race

1.5. Percent of American Adults who reached various Income Distribution over 44-year Period

1.6. Poverty Rate by Race from 2019 to 2020 using the Supplemental Poverty Measure

Chapter 2

2.0. U.S. States GDP Growth, 2006-2016

2.1. Growth of Food Stamps Recipients, 2007, 2016

2.2. Average SAT Score for Admitted Students to Harvard by Race

2.3. Experience with Discrimination by Birth Race

2.4. Educational Attainment by Race in 2015

2.5. Median Household Income by Race in 2020

2.6. Median Household between Indians and Asians Living in the United States in 2019

Chapter 3

3.0. Means-Tested Welfare or Aid to the Poor

3.1. Percent of U.S. Births out-of-wedlock by Major Racial Group, 1964 -2014

3.2. Median Family Wealth by Race, 1992-2016

3.3. Effect of Hypothetical Implementation of a $9.00 minimum wage on Black Teenagers

Chapter 4

4.0. Rate of Illiteracy of the Black Community, 1870-1960

4.1. Impact of Black Illiteracy Rate on Black Employment in the Agricultural Sector, 1870-1964

4.2. Judicial Compensation in 2022

4.3. Single-Parenthood by Race and Gender in 2018

4.4. Rates of new HIV Diagnoses per 100,000 by Race in 2018

4.5. HIV Death Rate in the United States in 2019 by Race

Chapter 5

5.0. Impact of Social Cost on Wealth Production

5.1. Assessment on Why it may be Harder for black people to get a ahead

5.2. Favorability Rating of Vice President Kamala Harris in the United States as of December 2021

5.3. Favorability Rating of Kamala Harris by Gender as of December 2021

5.4. Favorability Rating of Kamala Harris by Race as of December 2021

6.0. John Lewis's Salary, 1987-2020

Chapter 6

6.1. Business Ownership by Race, 2010-2019

6.2. Status of Business Equity Ownership in the United States, by Race

6.3. Homeownership by Race, 1994-2020

6.4. Share with Asset by Race

6.5. Average Value of Stockownership by Race

6.6. Functional Financial Knowledge for Black Americans

6.7. Impact of Educational Attainment of Blacks on Black Households Owning Stocks

Chapter 7

7.0. Median Value of Assets Held by Different Racial and Ethnic Groups

7.1. Average Credit Score by Racial Groups

7.2. Community-based Infrastructural Development Model

Chapter 8

8.0. Prevalence Rate of violent Crime in the United States from 2014 to 2019 by Race/Ethnivity

8.1. Chicago Violent Crime 2019 versus 2020

8.2. Percentage of Gang Members by Age, 2019

8.3. Impact of Youth Unemployment on Crime in Chicago

8.4. Racial and Ethnic Disparities in High Youth Unemployment Areas, 2020

8.5. Fatal Police Shooting and Population Size by Ethnic Group

8.6. Number of People shot to death by the police in the United States from 2017 to 2021, by Race

8.7. Views on Police Performance by Race

8.8. Perceptions of Police Bias

8.9. Policing in Affluent Neighborhoods

8.10. Policing in Low-Income Black Neighborhoods

8.11. Inmate Population by Race, 2022

8.12. Average Rate of Imprisonment per 100,000 Residents, by 2019

8.13. Police Treatment by Race, 2020

Chapter 9

9.0. Median Income by Educational Attainment

Chapter 10

10.0. Declining White Population

Tables

Chapter 1

1.0. Poverty Measure Concepts: Official and Supplemental

Chapter 4

4.0. Hip-hop Artists Salary

Chapter 8

8.0. Paradigm of Street Organization

Chapter 9

9.0. Household Income Distribution

Printed in Great Britain
by Amazon